THE MUSICIAN'S GUIDE TO INDEPENDENT RECORD PRODUCTION

THE MUSICIAN'S GUIDE TO INDEPENDENT RECORD PRODUCTION

by Will Connelly

Contemporary Books, Inc.
Chicago

Library of Congress Cataloging in Publication Data

Connelly, Will.
    The musician's guide to independent record production.

    Includes index.
    1. Sound recording industry—United States.
I. Title.
ML3790.C69   338.4′778991′0973   80-68595
ISBN 0-8092-5969-9
ISBN 0-8092-5968-0 (pbk.)

Published by Contemporary Books, Inc.
180 North Michigan Avenue, Chicago, Illinois 60601
Manufactured in the United States of America
Library of Congress Catalog Card Number: 80-68595
International Standard Book Number: 0-8092-5969-9 (cloth)
                                                      0-8092-5968-0 (paper)

Published simultaneously in Canada by
Beaverbooks
953 Dillingham Road
Pickering, Ontario L1W 1Z7
Canada

To Tom Justice, Billy Butterfield, Frank Hubbell, and Don Goldie, the trumpet men who perpetuate the glorious memories of Bix, Louis, and Bobby; to Don Ewell, Jack Keller, Eddie Higgins, Bobby Rosen, and Harry Epp, incomparable jazz pianists; to clarinetist Ernie Goodson, Hank Bredenberg (trombone), "Red" Hawley (drums), and bassist Tom Sheeder, who spark the irresistible *Biscayne Jazz Band;* to S. H. T. Nelson, whose engineering skills defy comparison; to the Farrells, Ruth and Jim, who must be the world's most loyal and supportive jazz fans; to WPBT-TV for airing *Some of That Jazz,* and to the parade of disc jockeys led by WSBR's Jeff Rudolph for their contributions to the jazz heritage; and to Aileen, without whom there wouldn't be as much music in my life.

Contents

Session Direction • Mixdown and Editing • Production
Wrap-up • Test Record Approval

Preface

You can make records!

Maybe you're a rock/jazz/classical/bluegrass/pop/gospel/country-western instrumentalist or singer with unheralded talent. The first record you make could be the breakthrough you need.

Possibly you're a high school band director or a church choirmaster. The records you make and sell in your own community might pay for new uniforms for your kids, a new organ, or a trip to a music festival or band competition for your group.

Perhaps you're a doctor, lawyer, or Indian chief with unexploited musical gifts—or with the ability to recognize those gifts in others and to promote them through record making.

You can make records for fun, fame, or fortune. If you have solid musical talent, or you know someone who does, and if your musical tastes are similar to those of the general public, there's nothing to keep you from making records that have the sound of gold—records that can soar to the top of the sales charts to win you the coveted golden record plaques that mark hits which have touched multitudes of individuals, moved them to listen, and stimulated them to buy. If you make a really spectacular record, it could even "go platinum!"*

Whether you seek a shot at international stardom or want the extra income provided by selling records when your band performs at nightclubs, your record-making goal is feasible. If you are the individual who plans, organizes, and manages the process of putting out the record, you'll be what the industry calls an *independent record producer*. You'll be considered independent because you're not on the payroll of one of the major record companies.

The steps involved in making a record are the same whether you're an independent producer or an employee of one of the big-name labels. Your record will begin with an idea—an idea for a new song or a new sound, or a fresh approach to previously recorded material. Whatever your idea is, you'll be convinced that it is one that will appeal to the particular audience at which you are aiming.

Once you have an idea, you will develop a plan for making the record, organize the musicians and the music they are to play, and pick the studio and supervise the recording session. Along the way, you will work with graphic artists, who will design your labels and jackets; the mastering laboratory, which transfers your tape to a master disc; and others who will be members of your production team.

This book is intended to light the path you will follow and show you the steps you will take as you travel from your germinal idea for a record to the finished plastic discs or ribbons of tape through which you've brought that idea to maturity and immortalized it.

---

*The Recording Industry Association of America (RIAA) awards gold records for certified sales of a half million albums or tapes or one million singles. The platinum record plaque is awarded if album or tape sales exceed one million units.

There are many steps in the process of creating a record, but none of them is too complex for you to master with ordinary intelligence and common sense. To be a producer, you don't have to be a musician or an audio engineer, or even understand the intimate details of how records are manufactured. You will need to know how to find and use all the human and physical resources that are available to you in the recording industry, how to lead and direct the people on your production team, and how to plan and control your budget. All of these subjects and more are discussed in the chapters that follow.

Not only can you make records; *you couldn't have chosen a better time to do so.*

There's a larger audience for music than ever before, and people spend more money on records than on any other kind of entertainment. Radio and television, coupled with records, make it possible for music to leap over oceans and national boundaries. There are more good musicians alive today than ever before in history. Many—perhaps most—have yet to be discovered; some of the talent in local high school bands and at colleges is simply awesome. And what a time for new ideas! A great deal of enormously popular music is being played today on electronic instruments that didn't even exist a decade ago.

It's a time of opportunity—of golden (maybe even platinum!) opportunity—and if you have musical ideas to share, you not only *can* make records, you *should*. As a musician and fellow producer I hope you do, and I'll be listening.

I thank Bob Crothers of the American Federation of Musicians, Paul Burket of the American Federation of Television and Radio Artists, producer Dave Pell, Jack Davis of Criteria Recording, Wayne Heiser of Handleman Company, and Mr. Westermann of Southern Machine and Tool Company for their valued contributions to this volume.

Will Connelly
Plantation, Florida
June 1980

1

Introduction

As the eighties begin, the record industry is on the verge of becoming a $5-billion-a-year business in the United States, which means that it accounts for more entertainment revenues than the movies and more than all spectator sports combined. As one industry executive puckishly notes, it is "larger than the gross national product of Burma." And, even though the United States is the largest single market in the world, it represents only about a third of the total international record market.

The business is supported by record companies, recording studios, pressing plants and tape duplicators, jobbers and distributors, and retail stores. All of these functions, and still others, depend for their success on a mystical, intangible rapport between creative artists and the multitudes that make up the buying public.

Ever since the phonograph became a universal household appliance, the best-selling music has been contemporary in style: jazz in the twenties, swing in the thirties, pop in the forties, and rock in its various forms from the fifties through the present. But there has always been some market for all music—from classical to country, from accordion to zither— and it is through the quest to tap these markets, large and small, that thousands of new records are produced every year.

The record business includes two markedly different kinds of producing activities.

First, there are the major labels. These are the few very large companies—such as RCA, Warner's, and Columbia—which do millions of dollars worth of business annually. The product lines of the major labels tend to span the entire gamut of music from the classics to jazz, rock, country, and all the other forms. The major labels tend to be integrated vertically, owning their own studios, pressing plants, and distribution facilities.

The other activities that produce records are the independent labels. Some approach the major labels in business volume, but most are smaller. The independents tend to concentrate on one particular category of music, such as jazz, and seldom produce records outside the range of their main interests. Independents generally do not own recording studios; their records and tapes are manufactured by other companies under contract, and their distribution and marketing are almost always handled by independent distributors and rack jobbers.

The major labels dominate the market; some estimates attribute 85 percent of all sales to them. This fact apparently did not daunt Herb Alpert, a musician and recording studio engineer who parlayed the sound of his Tijuana Brass into A&M Records, the largest of the independents with annual sales of about $100 million.

The record industry is unique in that it allows giants and small independents to coexist and to compete with each other. This is possible because there is no monopoly on creativity, which is the keystone of the business. As Alpert and others have repeatedly shown, it is entirely possible for a talented musician, singer, or group of musicians with a bright new idea to strike a responsive chord with the public and to turn out a record that sells millions of copies on an initial investment of a few thousand dollars. In 1979 one such winner was *Lots More Crude or No More Food,* a seriocomic country-western piece that expressed the national "up in arms" sentiment about the OPEC-inspired oil crisis.

It is also possible to fail in the record business and, depending on the kind of material being tried, the odds against recovering the costs of production can run as high as ten to one.

The major labels reduce, but by no means eliminate, risks in the same way that television producers do—by imitating successes. When disco records began to sell in significant quantities in the mid-seventies, the rush was on and labels raced to cut 120-beat-per-minute thumpers that were only barely distinguishable from one another. While a great deal of money was made by those who participated in the disco explosion, it is likely that some latecomers—as well as many others who pressed huge quantities of disco records in mid-1979—were hurt badly when disco's popularity plummeted in late '79. Timing is every bit as important as correctly identifying which bandwagon to board.

Two other mechanisms help reduce risk. One is the use of name talent—each monster Bee Gees record spawns its own successors. The other is heavy "act" promotion, now waning, in which major labels spend massive amounts to develop new groups and send them on concert tours.

Few independent labels can afford star talent with name recognition or the huge expense of advance national promotion that will develop unknown talent into national figures before the first record is released. If these were the only ways to break into the business, the capital requirements would be so great that they would preclude the existence of independent labels. There are two characteristics of the business that leave apertures for success to independent, even very small, labels. First, radio air play, which is the most important tool of all for promotion, is free. Second, independent distributors are available to get the records to the buying public through retail record stores. A record based on a good idea combined with good talent can still make it, and even make it big, in the record business without stars or broad advance promotion, even though it is a risky proposition.

The mass market record game is a mix of art, technology, and commerce that is played on the unpredictable, volatile, and fickle field of public taste, and even the Goliaths in the business can guess wrong. The bad guesses are largely found in the "cut-out" bins of retail record stores, where albums sell for as low as 99¢.

Not every record that is made is aimed at the mass public market. The conductor of a church choir may make an album of the choir with a view to raising funds for a new organ through sales to the congregation. Or the director of the high school band may make a record in the hope that sales will pay for new uniforms. The leader of a popular local band may cut a record that can be sold at live nightclub and concert appearances. When records are made for purposes like these, for a well-defined and virtually guaranteed market, albeit a small one, there's practically no risk of failure.

From concept to cashbox, the steps involved in making a record are the same, whether the record ultimately sells one copy or millions. The steps, and the participants in the game, are shown in Figure 1.

Every record starts with a concept that defines what the finished product is supposed to be. The concept will typically identify music, musicians, a desired sound, how the product will be released (record, tape, or both), and indicate why it is marketable.

The concept may have been generated by management or brought to management by an outsider (often a producer). If the project goes ahead, management will have to supply some important services, such as accounting, legal services, purchasing, marketing, and business interaction with unions, music "mechanical rights" licensors, and the Copyright Office of the Library of Congress.

Before any actual work is done on a record project, management will do two things that do not appear in Figure 1: it will develop a budget to see how much the project will cost, and it

FIGURE 1
The Record-Making Process, from Concept to Cashbox

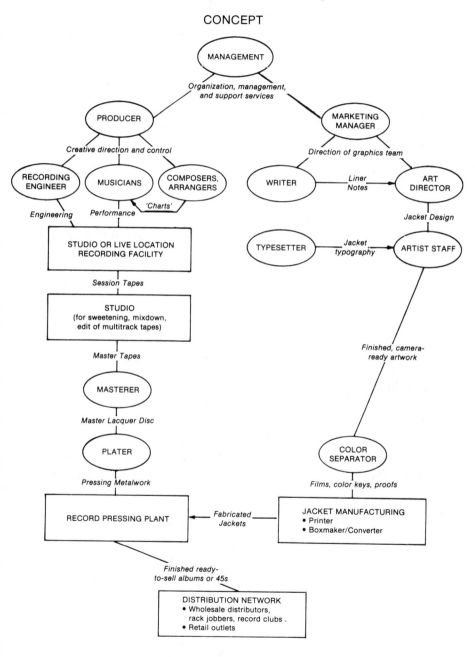

will either invest or raise the capital necessary to finance the effort. The producer and artists are usually participants in, or at least contributors of information to, the budgeting and financing processes.

At this point the business splits into two separate functions: music production, headed by a producer; and graphics production—album jackets, labels, tape cartons, and the like—which is usually managed by the marketing department or the ad agency. The end product of the producer's work is a master disc or tape that can be used to manufacture either records or tapes. The marketing manager's output is camera-ready artwork that can be used to manufacture all the packaging.

On the music production side, the producer supervises the efforts of music writers and arrangers who create the music, the musicians and vocalists who will perform it in their own creative way, and the audio engineers who do the recording. The producer will supervise the recording sessions—one or several, in one or several locations; will supervise mixdown or remix sessions; and will select and edit from recorded tape to assemble the best possible master.

On the graphics production end, the marketing, advertising, or graphics manager will work with an art director—and, if liner notes are to appear on a jacket, with a writer—to come up with a package concept. Artists, typographers, photographers, and layout people may all contribute to the finished artwork.

At this point the creative work on the record is done, with the exception of the work done by the mastering laboratory on a disc end product. What remains are the manufacturing processes to generate volume quantities of the record and the package it will be sold in.

If the end product is to be cassette or eight-track tapes, the master tape goes to a tape duplicating house that makes copies in volume. The master tape is played back at many times its original recorded speed while from several to dozens of cassettes or cartridges are recorded simultaneously, also at higher than normal speed.

If a disc is the end product, the master tape is used to make a lacquer disc master at the mastering laboratory. This disc recording goes to a specialty electroplater that makes the matrices—one matrix for each side of the disc—or metalwork, from which the records are stamped, or pressed, by the pressing plant.

While the records or tapes are being made, the finished artwork goes to a photographic specialty house at which lithographic negatives and/or color separations are made. From these films, printing plates are made and jackets or boxes are turned out in volume by the printer. The printed product goes to a boxmaker or paper converter (sometimes) for final assembly, and the finished printed matter goes to the duplicator or pressing plant, where it is stuffed with the music product and sealed in plastic shrink wrap.

When the records or tapes are finished, management will send off copies, with an application for copyright, to the Library of Congress's Copyright Office.

At this point, with hundreds or thousands of ready-to-sell discs and/or tapes sitting on the manufacturing plant's shipping dock, the producing label had better have the mechanisms in place to get those records to the buying public. If the records were intended for some specific local market, as many fund-raising records are, they're sold more or less like Girl Scout cookies to friends, relatives, members of the congregation, and the like. But if the idea is to sell the record to the public at large, the label should have its distribution established and should be prepared to promote and market its product. Merchandising is the term that includes selling, credit management, and such promotional activities as getting radio air play and TV exposure and doing concerts.

Some major record companies own most of the facilities needed to produce, manufacture, and merchandise records they make, such as recording studios, pressing plants, printing plants and branch distribution warehouses. Nearly all other companies make use of independent facilities. Recording studios are available for rent throughout the world. Independent, and even major-company, pressing plants, will press records for anyone, including competitors. Independent specialty companies handle plating, graphic arts, printing, duplicating, and everything else necessary to manufacture record products. Independent regional and national distributors, serving dozens of major and independent record labels, sell records to retail record stores and other outlets, such as supermarkets, drugstores, and chain stores.

Although major labels often have their own studio facilities and pressing plants, it is another unique characteristic of the business that majors frequently have records produced in outside studios and turn unhesitatingly to outside pressing plants when their own plants are overloaded. Also, an independent label can do its recordings in major label studios if it so desires, and it may have a major label pressing plant manufacture its records. Independent distributors and rack jobbers handle products from both majors and independent labels, and some major label branch operations distribute for independent labels. The industry is so structured that every essential service is available to all comers at essentially the same prices. This odd feature of the business is another factor that makes it possible to get started with relatively little capital, and to be extremely successful if the concept is good.

The record business, like other segments of the entertainment industry, can be fun. But if record making is to be profitable, it has to be approached as a business in which the objective is to create a salable product at an affordable cost and, of particular importance, at a cost that is affordable even if the record is a flop. The record business is a little like Las Vegas: there's lots of glitter, flash, and romance, but every bet includes the genuine risk that the house will rake in the chips.

2

Record-Making Technology and Processes

While the technical side of record making is generally the province of those involved in engineering and manufacturing, administrators and producers need to have a basic understanding of the nuts and bolts of the business, since technical options can greatly influence managerial and creative decisions. It is equally helpful to understand the arcane vocabulary of the craft.

The end products of the record business are the 7-inch 45 rpm single, the twelve-inch 33⅓ rpm long-playing album, the ⅛-inch tape cassette or the ¼-inch tape eight-track cartridge. The production process is essentially the same for any of these deliverable product formats, but only the manufacturing and packaging are different.

RECORDING

Before the invention of the tape recorder, music was picked up from the live performing group and was recorded directly on the soft-lacquer-faced master disc. The recordings were single-channel monaural. All instruments and vocalists were picked up by carefully placed microphones, and the recording engineer mixed for the proper blend (balance or mix) of sounds and for the proper volume (level) as the master disc was being cut. Performers were challenged to run through a complete performance without musical error, and the engineer was challenged to do so without technical error.

In effect, all recording was done direct-to-disc, a technique that is enjoying a renaissance because it results in discs with the best fidelity and noise characteristics consonant with (limited) volume manufacture.

The introduction of professional quality tape recorders in the early fifties had two technical effects of profound creative impact: the ability to edit and multitrack capability. If a performance was good except for some small glitch—a misplayed note, for example—only a brief segment of the performance had to be repeated and recorded on a fresh tape. The defective segment would be edited out of the tape and the corrected segment would be spliced in, exactly as with motion picture film. The first effect of the ability to record more than one track on the tape, for which there was then no existing practical disc equivalent, was to permit binaural (later stereo) recording.

The original stereo recorders recorded two independent tracks on ¼-inch tape. The next step was three tracks on ½-inch tape. As the ability to manufacture more compact and precision heads for tape recorders developed, machine technology evolved to the present point at which forty tracks can be recorded on 2-inch tape. This development made it possible to assign one or more microphones to each instrument or voice in fairly large groups and to record the sounds from each microphone on its own individual channel on the tape. The final sound balance (mix) could now be done as the original recording was played back, rather than during recording. The producer and engineer gained the opportunity to make balance refinements at leisure rather than in real time, as the performance occurred, and thus was born the phrase "We'll fix it in the mix," or mixdown, as the process is called.

A related benefit was the ability to erase the performance of a single player or singer, instead of the whole group, and have that performer repeat and correct his or her performance as it was rerecorded, or overdubbed, on the vacated (erased) track. Finally, as multichannel machines were installed in studios throughout the world, it became possible to "lay the rhythm tracks" in Hollywood, send the tape to New York to have a hot lead guitarist add a part, then send the tape to Memphis for the addition of vocals, and finally send it back to Hollywood for special effects, sweetening, and mixdown. Many modern records have been made by performers who have never met each other.

These benefits are not without penalty. Before multitrack, the tape of a performance in which all the sounds were pre-mixed during the performance became the master tape. With multitrack, the master tape that is sent to the mastering laboratory is a mixed-down copy of the original live performance tape and is one step removed from the live performance. Each successive step, or generation, between the original perfor-mance and the final delivered-to-the-consumer phonograph record or tape results in perceptible degradation of sound quality.

After a brief technical and marketing battle between com-peting methods, the Westrex method of stereo disc recording was adopted as the industry standard in preference to a system proposed by Columbia Records. Technical discussion on these methods will be found in the reference volumes listed in the bibliography; in essence, however, a stereo disc recording is a two-channel device. Eventually, all the channels of the live recording and any intermediate processing must wind up in the two channels available on the disc or on cassette and cartridge tapes. The master tape sent to the mastering lab that will cut the lacquer masters, or to the tape duplicator that will manu-facture cassettes and cartridges, is a two-channel tape.

An exception to the foregoing is that some mastering labs

accepted four-track masters during the brief period in which it appeared that quadraphonic four-channel technology might become a commercial success. It didn't and will not be discussed further here.

The direct-to-disc technique described earlier is likely to enjoy only a transient resurrection. The reason for this is that a new digital recording technology is evolving rapidly. Through this method, the performance material, which is analog data, is sampled and transformed into the same kind of electrical digital signal that is used in computers. Digital recording promises all the benefits of multitrack recording with none of the fidelity or signal-to-noise degradation associated with conventional analog recording as successive generations are made. Digital recording is still experimental and probably several years away from widespread availability in studios.

Until there is another dramatic change in the recording industry, similar to those which occurred when 45s and LPs replaced 78 rpm records, or when stereo was introduced to the consumer, the end product of a record production effort will continue to be the two-channel master tape, whether that recording is analog or digital.

DISC MASTERING AND MANUFACTURING

The two-track master tape is transferred to a lacquer master disc on a recording lathe at the mastering laboratory. The master lacquer, which may be the original of a direct-to-disc session, is then sensitized, typically in a silver nitrate solution or by vacuum deposition, to produce a microscopically thin metallic coating. That coating conforms to the lands and grooves of the recorded material and is electroplated with nickel to a substantial thickness, about $3/_{32}$ inch. The metal part is carefully separated from the lacquer master, which, after this process, is rarely usable for the production of more plated-up metal parts.

The metal part that has been separated from the lacquer master is a reverse image of the lacquer; the lacquer grooves become lands and vice versa. This metal part is the metal master, and it can be used in either of two ways.

For a short manufacturing run, the metal master can be used as a stamper; it is inserted into the record-making press, which, when fed with vinyl and the labels for the record, makes the actual manufactured disc. One stamper is required for each side of the record.

Alternatively, the metal master can be used to make additional metal parts by sensitizing and plating processes similar to those used to create the metal master from the lacquer master. These new parts are called mothers. Having once again undergone land and groove reversal in the duplicating process, the mothers are positive images of the original lacquer master. As such, they can't be used to press records because the lands and grooves would be reversed in the resultant product. The mothers are used to make yet another set of metal parts, once more in reverse image, which are the stampers for large production runs.

The process is illustrated in Figure 2.

It is evident that both the manner of original recording and the number of records to be manufactured have an effect on the sound quality of the final disc product. The sound quality decreases as the quantity increases in any of the steps involved: records produced from the fifth stamper manufactured from the fifth mother will not be as good as those produced from some earlier members of the same mother and stamper generations; also, the last record pressed from that stamper will not be as good as the first. The reasons for diminishing quality is the development of pits during successive plating operations. These are slight deformations that occur during successive separations of metal copies from the parts from which they were copied. Simple wear and accumulations of microscopic dirt or chemical residue on the stampers can also contribute to lower quality.

Two other points should be observed with regard to the technology of record making.

First, while quality of manufacture can be assured by such

FIGURE 2
Generations between Performance and Final Disc Product

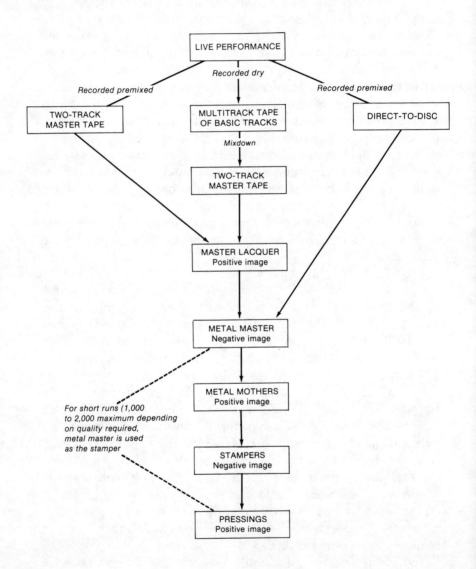

techniques as cutting duplicate masters, pressing only from metal masters, and limiting the number of parts made from each predecessor part, the cost will increase for each such quality control step imposed.

Second, at least until digital recording is widely and economically available, there is a significant quality advantage to recording live two-track tape if it is creatively feasible to do so. It makes no sense, for example, to record a piano soloist on multitrack. A possible collateral factor is that the very discipline involved in recording good live two-track originals—not as rigid as direct-to-disc but much more so than multitrack— may result in substantial cost savings. This is due to the fact that both the opportunity and the temptation to strive for nearly inaudible perfections in long mixdown sessions is eliminated.

TABLE 1

If the Master Delivered to the Electroplater Is	And the Manufacturing Run Is	The Final Disc Is
1. A direct-to-disc lacquer	Short*	Third generation
2. A lacquer mastered from a two-track original live tape recording	Short	Fourth generation
3. Same as (2)	Long	Sixth generation
4. A lacquer mastered from a mixed-down two-track copy of a multitrack original	Short	Fifth generation
5. Same as (4)	Long	Seventh generation

*Long runs are not possible.

DISC TIME LIMITATIONS

It is possible to record a maximum of about 30 minutes of program material on each side of a twelve-inch LP, and maximum playing time was once considered a major objective in album recording. Two technical factors influence maximum available disc program time. One is the dynamic range of the recorded material—the difference between the highest sound intensity and the amount of residual noise left in an unmodulated groove. The other is allowable distortion—the deviation between the original program material and what can be achieved in playback.

High dynamic range requires increased average distance between adjacent grooves in the record to accommodate the greater lateral excursions of the cutting, and thus playback, styli. Greater spacing reduces the lineal length of the groove and, thus, playing time.

Lowest attainable distortion, along with best overall frequency response, occurs at the start of the recorded groove. As the groove spirals inward toward the label, distortion increases and response falls. The last audio modulation should occur at or before an inside groove radius of 4¾ inches. The groove is then spiraled out and locked to finish the cut and to provide a rapid change in horizontal velocity that can be sensed by the trip mechanisms in automatic turntables.

Jack Davis of Criteria Records ("The Home of the Bee Gees"), which is both a recording studio and a mastering laboratory, states that the absolute maximum time limits consistent with reasonably acceptable signal-to-noise ratio and distortion are shown in Table 2.

For some of the really extreme rock material, it is desirable to reduce the time even more to permit deeper and more widely spaced grooves, which help cheap phonograph pickup arms track without jumps or skips.

CASSETTE AND CARTRIDGE MANUFACTURE

Both cassettes and cartridges contain tapes that are dupli-

TABLE 2

	Seven-inch	Twelve-inch
For speech and musical material of sharply limited dynamic range	5 minutes	28 minutes
For middle-of-the-road background music with moderate dynamic range	4½ minutes	24 minutes
For rock and disco or any material with a high bass or percussive content	4 minutes	22 minutes

cated from submaster tapes that are first generation, or no more than second generation, copies of the final production master tape.

It is not practical to record copy tapes (the cassettes or cartridges) in real time, that is, at the same speed as the original material. To do so would mean that making each cassette or cartridge would take 35 to 45 minutes on the duplicating machine and that the tape duplicating process would be prohibitively expensive even when a single submaster tape feeds the program material to banks of simultaneously recording duplicating machines. The solution to this problem has been to speed up both the submaster tape and the tapes being duplicated to several times original speed, which reduces duplicating time by the speed increase factor. The current speed factor is as high as sixty-four, so that actual tape recording time for a cassette containing forty minutes of material can be as low as 37.5 seconds (compared with about 30 seconds to press a twelve-inch disc).

Cassette tapes are like reel-to-reel tapes of a given length and have a definite duration per side. Program material should be planned for as close to equal duration on each side of the tape as possible to avoid manufacturing waste.

Cartridge tapes are made as endless loops, so there is no technical reason why per-side length need be considered. Total time must be kept below forty minutes. After the tape has made one complete pass through the playback machines, the play heads are rapidly and automatically shifted to pick up the next pair of tracks. This process is repeated until all four pairs of tracks have been played. Good creative planning, however, makes it desirable to have the total program divided into four sides so that the track changeover occurs between, rather than during, selections.

With both cassettes and cartridges, the extremely high-speed duplication technique that increases production and cuts manufacturing cost is accompanied by serious losses of fidelity. Consumers with good high-fidelity equipment report that many current tape products are inferior to disc pressings of the same material.

GLOSSARY

Some of the terms that are frequently heard in the studio are defined below.

Board. This is the mixing console to which microphones and electronic instruments are connected. The board's output feeds the recording equipment, monitor speaker amplifiers, and the performer's headphones. Internal switching can route signals from individual or mixed channels to outboard processors, such as echo chambers. The board is also used to recombine the many tracks of a multitrack recording back down to the two channels that exist in a master tape.

dB, or decibel. A term used to define increases or decreases in electrical or acoustical signal strengths. Mathematically, an acoustical (sound pressure level) or voltage ratio expressed in dB is twenty times the logarithm (base ten) of the ratio. An electrical power ratio is, in dB, ten times the log of the ratio. Most of the decibel indicating meters in studios are connected to voltage-source circuits. To a crude approximation, sound from the monitor speakers that is twice or half as loud as some prior reference is said to be up 6 dB or down 6 dB, respectively. A ten-time change would be 20 dB. Equalization changes (below) are also expressed in dB, as, for example, "boost the midrange 3 dB."

Desk. Same as **Board.**

Direct box. This device, which contains amplifiers and/or impedance transformers and/or isolation transformers, permits the output of an electronic instrument (e.g., synthesizer), an instrument amplifier, or the pickup built into instruments such as guitars, to be fed directly into the board. Direct boxes are used as alternatives or supplements to microphones placed in front of the instrument or its amplifier loudspeaker. Using a direct box eliminates the acoustical crosstalk, in which the sound from some other instrument in the studio is picked up by a microphone for an instrument that is direct-boxed. Direct boxes are frequently used when the instrumental sound is to undergo some sort of processing (e.g., echo) before it is recorded and when dry tracks are being sought.

Dry tracks. Recording to produce the least possible crosstalk from one recorded track of a multitrack recording to another, for the purpose of affording the greatest flexibility during mixdown, is called recording dry tracks. Dry tracks are recorded in acoustically "dead" studios, with as much physical separation between instruments that are miked (as differentiated from those fed to the board from direct boxes) as possible. The drummer works in an acoustically absorbent drum booth. A piano is often covered with acoustically absorbent batting or blankets or a shroud. Performers listen to the sounds being produced on headphones rather than via the direct acoustical path. Dry tracks have little or none of the luster or ambiance of sound picked up by microphones in a more lively (reverberant) environment, but they are easy to augment electronically.

Dub, dubbing. When a disc or tape is copied (rerecorded) on another disc or tape, the copy is called a dub. In multitrack recording, material from one track can be dubbed from one track to another (called a *bounce*). If material previously recorded on a given track is erased as new material is simultaneously recorded, the process is called overdubbing.

Echo. See **Reverb**.

Equalization (EQ). Each input channel on the board is usually equipped with one or more controls that permit the frequency response curve of that channel to be modified. For high-voiced instruments—piccalos, for example—the low frequency end of the channel spectrum may be cut to reduce the pickup and crosstalk from basses and drums.

Flanging, Fuzzing, Phasing. These are electrical or electromechanical techniques for altering the character of sound. Flanging and phasing create a sound kindred to echo, but with the echo occurring variably at different frequencies in a slow "wow-wow" pattern. Fuzzing distorts sounds to produce a buzzing or raspy effect. These effects and many others are extensively used in rock and disco and to lesser degrees in other musical forms.

Gain. This term refers to the amount of amplification of an electrical signal. The volume control on a radio could also be called a gain control. Gain is commonly discussed and measured in decibels.

Level. Electrical signal levels, expressed often in decibels. Level is often used interchangeably with gain.

Mute. A switch provided for each channel on the board which permits that channel to be silenced without having to alter the gain setting for the channel. Often used in mixdown to keep a channel dead until the associated track contains desired signal (e.g., mute until a recorded vocal comes up on the track).

Reverb(eration). Reverb is used to refer to most devices or techniques that produce an echolike effect, including actual echo chambers, echo plates, spring/transducer echo devices, digital delay lines, and multihead tape machines. The various reverb-producing technologies all have different echo-simulating abilities and musical character.

Riding gain. This is the process of making gain adjustments to individual channels or groups of channels as a performance is recorded or mixed down.

Solo. Most modern boards have a solo capability that permits the engineer to put the output from any individual channel into the monitoring speakers without affecting the gain setups for that or any other channel. It is a diagnostic tool that can be used during recording without affecting the material being recorded.

TECHNICAL REFERENCES

Other technical terms will be used and described in the text as appropriate. For definitions of these, and for technical details, the following references are recommended.

Sound Recording, by John Eargle (Van Nostrand Reinhold Company, 450 W. 33rd St., New York, NY 10001). This book was written by a leading recording engineer and is aimed primarily at other engineers. However, it is so well written that nonengineers will be able to understand a great deal of the information presented.

Handbook of MultiChannel Recording, by Alton Everest (TAB Books, Blue Ridge Summit, PA 17214). Everest, another top recording engineer, has written with considerably more emphasis on practice and application than Eargle. Specific technical hardware is discussed and illustrated.

Audio Cyclopedia, by Howard Tremain (Howard W. Sams, Indianapolis, IN 46268). This is the audio engineer's bible. It is a particularly useful reference work for the manager who wants to understand the engineering vocabulary that flies around the studio.

3

Administrative Functions in Record Production

As noted earlier, the craft of making records is a mix of creative, engineering, and business activities.

In major label companies, entire executive contingents and staffs are given responsibilities for general management, accounting, legal affairs, purchasing, manufacturing, and marketing activities that are more or less separate from production but of vital concern from a production viewpoint. There is a great deal of interdependency: what happens in the administrative end of the business can affect the production side, and vice versa.

Whether the independent label organization is a formally structured corporation or simply a group of musicians who have decided to cut a record for nightclub sales, the administrative functions have to be performed. This can be handled through delegation to outside specialists such as lawyers and accountants or to other members of the organization who have the ability to take on the duties. This chapter will discuss what needs to be done administratively, primarily in the context of the relationship to production.

FINANCE

It takes money to make records, and at least part of that money has to be raised before anything else can happen. The amount of money (capital) that has to be raised depends on the answers to many questions, including, but by no means limited to, the following.

- How much will be paid to performers for recording, and how much can (and should) be deferred and paid as royalties from money derived through sales?
- How much studio time will it take to create the master tapes, and what will that cost?
- How many records will be manufactured initially to provide an inventory from which revenue-producing sales can be made?

Determining the amount to be raised is part of what preparing a budget is all about; budgeting will be discussed in a later chapter. There is no point in beginning a record project if there's a possibility that the available funds won't be sufficient to finish it.

Established record companies can look to the accumulated profits from previous records to finance new projects. New production organizations—companies, partnerships, or individuals—will have to find other sources. In order of increasing difficulty of access, such sources include the following:

- Personal savings.
- Loans collateralized by property other than the master tapes and records to be produced (e.g., a second mortgage on a home).
- Offering shares of future profits to active participants (e.g., musicians in a group), relatives, and friends, either infor-

mally or through shareholdings in a corporation or partnership.

- Advances or loans from the agents of well-established and groups that have performed successfully but have not previously recorded.
- Financing by venture capital groups, often identified as Small Business Investment Corporations (SBICs) or Minority Enterprise Small Business Investment Corporations (MESBICs). Bankers, lawyers, accountants, and the Small Business Administration may provide leads to such sources.
- Bank financing collateralized by master tapes and/or manufactured product and/or copyrights on original material.
- Going public with the stock of a corporation.

Raising money is one of the most difficult steps for a recording company because the sales from which revenues will be raised to pay off loans and/or generate profits depend on the intangibles of public taste and merchandising. From a business viewpoint, record making is classed as a high-risk venture; an individual with less than a solid-gold track record in the business should expect to pay a very high price for money. That price is likely to include a substantial share of future profits, creative restrictions, tight accounting controls, or a security interest in masters, copyrights, and manufactured product, either alone or in some combination.

Professional musicians working a long engagement at a nightclub or other place have a built-in potential source of capital: the club ownership. A recording made by the appearing group enhances the club's prestige and, because the live audience is the best possible market for the records, recovery of costs through sales is virtually guaranteed over a period of time. Albums presently sell for $6 plus tax in clubs, and this revenue is not reduced by the usual costs of distribution. Each album sold is a permanent advertisement for the club, and the record itself can be produced inexpensively by taping it live at the club rather than in a studio.

Once money has been raised so that a project can begin, a

vital function of management is to act as a buffer between the financial sector and the creative personnel. In theory, once investors have funded a record project on the basis of a concept description supported by a budget, they should stand back and be satisfied to monitor progress through evaluation of periodic reports and to take substantive action to protect their investments only in the case of very material and serious problems in the creative process. As a practical matter, financial sources may prove to be motivated as much by an opportunity to be in "show biz" as by the actual economic potential of the venture. Management should generally expect more active interest from a record production investor than would be the case if the investment had been made to build a thumbtack factory. In dealing with this situation, management should try to accommodate the investor's personal interest without permitting it to intrude on the creative end.

ACCOUNTING

Sources of financing are entitled to, and generally will, require that all monies advanced be fully and properly accounted for. Equally important, up-to-date cost data are needed so that management can intervene promptly if there are any wild deviations from the preplanned budget or production schedule. Records will have to be kept to meet the requirements of tax authorities, to determine the cost of production, and to establish the depreciation base for tax purposes. Because events occur rapidly in some phases of record production, it is smart to keep a daily record of both actual and committed (accrued) expenses during high activity periods, and to furnish the producer with a daily summary of target costs versus actual costs to date.

If the production venture is anything other than a one-time deal intended to produce a record for some small-scale purpose (e.g., a demo), the accountant should consult with an attorney who is a specialist in entertainment business tax law. This is done to ensure that the books and records are kept and the accounting is done in a manner that will take full advantage of the tax shelters that are unique to this business. Such an attorney should also be consulted whenever a substantial investment is involved.

LEGAL MATTERS

Before the production effort begins, the people involved should determine whether it is advantageous to set up a formal corporation, to establish a partnership, or simply to operate under some less formal but nevertheless written agreement. Other activities of a legal nature that may be involved in record production include music licensing, artist contracts, execution of labor and other related agreements, and the preparation and filing of copyrights for original material (both musical and graphic) and finished master tapes. Matters that are related to the conduct of business generally include decisions on insurance (general liability, property, workman's compensation, medical), local or state business licenses or permits, and reporting as required to the various agencies of government at all levels. As noted above, there may also be a legal/accounting interaction, especially with regard to taxation.

A particularly valuable guide to the legal convolutions of the record business is *This Business of Music* by attorneys Sidney Shemel and M. William Krasilovsky, published by Billboard Publications, One Astor Plaza, New York, NY 10036.

It is not absolutely necessary to engage a lawyer to handle all the legal aspects of record production; an individual or a group with a composite general experience in business management as well as common sense should be able to deal with many of the requirements. Professional counsel is, however, a good investment when significant amounts of money are involved or when any complicating factor, such as the need to negotiate an artist royalty contract with performers, comes into play.

PURCHASING

A new or small recording organization probably will not

have a formal purchasing agent or group but should be able to assign the detailed work of purchasing to someone other than the producer. Purchasing activities are divided into three segments: obtaining quotations, price lists, and estimates that are necessary for budget preparation; issuing purchase orders for studio services that reflect advance agreement on price and other details; and contracting for record or tape manufacture after the production work is completed.

The producer will almost always choose the studio(s) at which the production work will be done from advance knowledge of desirable facilities, or individual engineers, or both. A good producer will usually try to list several facilities that will be compatible with his or her requirements so that the company has some latitude in shopping for the best prices, terms, and conditions that conform to the producer's requirements.

When the decision to go ahead with the project is firm, the purchasing department should be sure that quotations are based on clear understandings of all terms, for both budget development purposes and as the basis for a subsequent purchase order. Factors to check include the following:

- Free time allowed at each session for band setup, warm-up, and prerecording rehearsal.
- Charges that will be made if a session has to be canceled and rescheduled, and the advance notice that is required to avoid these charges.
- Availability of the studio beyond minimum scheduled time, in the event that a session runs long.
- Overtime rates and when they apply.
- Cost of tape and whether the studio will permit the tape to be supplied by the company instead of by the studio.
- Assurances that any engineers with whom the producer wants to work will be assigned to the project if the studio is selected.

All of these matters should be referred to in the purchase order ultimately issued to the chosen studio.

The time and effort spent in getting advance quotations for as many of the cost items reflected in the budget as possible will pay off in the accuracy of the budget and the reduction of risk that it will be overrun by surprises.

The purchase order to the mastering lab should specify whether a reference lacquer is required (at extra cost). The master tape sent to either mastering labs or duplicating plants along with the purchase order should be accompanied by any notes the producer and the engineers have prepared regarding their desires or requirements.

Purchase orders to production facilities (pressing plants or tape duplicators) should specify price, delivery time, F.O.B. point, and any requirements for quality control/assurance and the agreement as to what is to occur if the requirements of the order are not met. No record should be released for full-scale production until test pressings have been received and played to determine that nothing went wrong in the mastering or plating operations.

The best-known source book for information on suppliers of goods and services for the record industry is the *International Buyer's Guide,* published annually by Billboard Publications, P.O. Box 2156, Radnor, PA 19089. This volume lists names and addresses of licensing organizations, record pressing and tape duplicating plants, printers that specialize in record product packaging, and even manufacturers of record and tape manufacturing equipment. Its value goes far beyond purchasing, however; it also lists the names and addresses of music industry lawyers, both U.S. and foreign, jobbers and distributors, and organizations involved in record promotion. The reader who decides not to produce records will also find the names and addresses of record companies to whom audition tapes may be sent. (Be sure to write first; many companies will not listen to unsolicited tapes.) Billboard also prints a studio directory annually.

In any local area, the telephone directory's Yellow Pages are a good source of studio names. *Recording Engineer/Producer* magazine, published by Recording & Broadcasting Publications, 1850

Whitley Ave., Hollywood, CA 90028, contains useful and current information about studios throughout the world. It is also a good source of information on contemporary recording technology and production techniques.

MERCHANDISING

While the ability to merchandise finished records successfully is crucially dependent on what happens in production, the selling, distribution arrangements, promotion, and credit management activities that constitute the major parts of the merchandising craft are essentially separate from production and are management responsibilities.

GRAPHICS PRODUCTION

A successful record album or tape often owes almost as much of its sales success to the package it comes in as to the music it contains. The design of album jackets and tape cartons is a management responsibility, and the execution is normally handled under the auspices of a marketing department, usually by an advertising agency and its art staff. The graphics manager will depend on the music producer for accurate time length for each record selection and for access to performers for photographs and collections of biographical data that may be used on liner notes or in later promotional efforts. The graphics manager will depend on legal personnel for precisely accurate song titles, names of composers/lyricists and publishers, and instructions on the use of trademark indicia, copyright notices, and warnings against unauthorized duplication that are to appear on labels, album jackets, and tape boxes. The graphics manager will design a logotype for the label if one does not already exist and may specify or recommend proper usage of the logo on company letterheads and advertising materials, as well as on the manufactured product.

If budget or market considerations either rule out or make it unnecessary to develop a custom jacket or box for the product, several pressing plants and specialty printing companies offer prefabricated jackets with stock pictures and graphics. These jackets and boxes are tailored to the individual album by overprinting the album name, artist information, and jacket-back liner notes. Some of the jackets also permit an artist photograph to appear on the front.

A well-conceived and well-executed jacket will not necessarily sell a record that has neither generated major retail sales nor been promoted extensively. But a shabby, unimaginative jacket *will* discourage sales. Until the music sells on its own merit, or as a result of advertising and promotion, the only factor on which a potential buyer can base a purchasing decision is the album jacket, with the information it contains and its aesthetic appeal.

More information on graphics preparation and fabrication is included in Chapter 5.

MUSIC MECHANICAL RIGHTS LICENSING

The composer of a piece of music has the right to secure a copyright of the work from the Register of Copyrights of the Library of Congress. Either the composer or the publisher will usually appoint a specialist organization to act as an agent, administrator, and collector of royalties that may be earned as a result of the protection the composer gets by copyrighting the work.

Permission to record a piece of music is called a *mechanical right* (a holdover from the early days of acoustical phonographs and player pianos) as differentiated from a performance right, which, for example, would be applicable if the music were done as part of a stage play. Under the Copyright Act of 1976, Congress established the rate structure for royalties that are payable if copyrighted material is recorded.

The specialist organizations that issue licenses to record music are called *mechanical rights licensors*. The major mechanical rights licensors in the United States are the Harry Fox Agency, 110 E. 59th St., New York, NY 10022; the American Mechanical Rights Association (AMRA), 250 W. 57th St., New York, NY 10019; and SESAC, 10 Columbus Circle, New York, NY 10019.

Obtaining mechanical rights licenses may not be the producer's direct responsibility, but a producer should be responsible for seeing to it that licenses have been obtained for any music that is to be recorded.

Not all music is subject to mechanical licensing requirements. If a song was first published or copyrighted in the United States before July 2, 1909, it is effectively in the public domain as far as the payment of royalties is concerned. However, it may not be in the public domain with respect to reproduction in print. Anything first published before September 20, 1906, is unrestrictedly in the public domain. No royalties are payable on the use of music that is in the public domain; the copyright owner's protection under the law has expired.

Music first published or copyrighted after the dates mentioned above may or may not be in the public domain, depending on whether or not the copyright was timely renewed at the end of the first of two twenty-eight-year periods originally specified in the pre-1976 Copyright acts, and on whether it fell under certain carry-over protections of the new 1976 act.

The obvious reason for using public domain music is that it reduces the cost of records sold. Whether that cost reduction makes any sense from an artistic viewpoint is, of course, a basic creative decision in forming the record concept.

The reason for obtaining a mechanical rights license to record copyrighted music is simply that failure to do so results in infringement of the copyright and lays the infringer open to legal action that can lead to fines, jail, and payment of either actual damages and profits or statutory damages and court costs under the Copyright Act of 1976. Even if a producer is an outside contractor, hired by a group of musicians or a company to produce a record on a one-shot basis, the producer is very likely to be one of the parties against whom the legal action is brought.

The best bet is to seek the license as soon as the music to be recorded is fully defined by the concept for the record. Submit a letter of request for the license to the Harry Fox Agency. List each song for which a license is sought, with the names of the writers, lyricists, and the publisher, if possible. Furnish the title of the proposed record if it's an album or tape. Give the name of the company or producer to whom the license is to be issued. The Fox Agency will issue a license to record all the songs for which they act on behalf of authors or publishers. If they cannot issue the license themselves, they will generally provide the name of another mechanical rights licensor who can. The record will then be covered by multiple licenses and, if any of the songs are in the public domain, Fox will generally advise you to that effect. However, be aware that a statement made by Fox or anyone else that a song is in the public domain should be taken merely as advice and not as a guarantee that the song is, in fact, in the public domain. In this event the producer will have to do research with the Register of Copyrights, at public libraries, with educational institutions, and so on, to determine absolutely that the song is in the public domain, or hire a research firm to do the legwork.

When the license is received, it should be checked very carefully against the title/author/publisher list originally supplied. Many songs have similar names, and the last thing a producer wants to do is to record a tune under a license that really applies to some other tune. The error might provide a defense in court, but the courtroom is not where the producer belongs.

The mechanical rights license will generally have the exact title of the song and the correct spellings of author and publisher names. Still, a producer is well advised to confirm the data on the license with any available alternative sources, such as a previous recording of the same tune or the sheet music. He or she should also have any ambiguities or errors corrected on the license before proceeding. When confirmed, the exact, correct information will also appear on record labels and/or jackets and/or boxes.

Many contemporary groups write their own music. Before

the music is recorded, the creators should copyright it and put in writing the agreement under which the material will be used in the record. The agreement can be whatever the parties want, including even a royalty-free license to record or the sale of the copyright to the recording company.

Under the Copyright Act of 1976, the holder of a copyright is not free to deny a license to anyone who wants to record the material. The act provides for a compulsory license and sets the maximum payment rates as follows:

> With respect to each work embodied in the phonorecord, the royalty shall be either two and three-fourths cents, or one-half cent per minute of playing time or fraction thereof, whichever amount is larger.

The royalty amount is payable for each record ultimately distributed. Failure to make the royalty payment when due effectively cancels the license and opens the door to infringement proceedings.

The rate structure above applies to compulsory licenses, that is, to licenses that must be granted to anyone willing to pay the rate. It may be possible to negotiate a lower rate with the licensor, but it will not be necessary to pay a higher rate.

The Copyright Tribunal, which has a Congressional mandate to review and change statutory rates periodically, met and held hearings with representatives of the music industry in the summer and fall of 1980. At the time this book was prepared, the Tribunal had not announced any alterations in the rates given above. Producers and administrators should determine whether or not rates have changed when planning and budgeting new productions.

The subject of copyrights is very complex, and it is well covered in terms that both laymen and businessmen can understand in the previously mentioned book, *This Business of Music*.

UNION "RECORDING LICENSE"

With exceptions, such as high school bands, recording musi-

cians will be members of the American Federation of Musicians
(AFM). Musicians who are union members are strictly prohib-
ited from recording unless the organization or individual to
whom they render services is a signatory to the Phonograph
Record Labor Agreement (PRLA) and the related Phonograph
Record Trust and Phonograph Record Manufacturers' Special
Payments Fund agreements. Musicians who violate the union
rules are subject to fines, expulsion, or both.

The Phonograph Record Labor Agreement contains the minimum wage scales payable to musicians, arrangers, and copyists
and establishes the work rules. These rules include but are not
confined to the length of a recording session and the amount of
music that may be recorded during the session, overtime, and
reimbursement for travel and cartage (the amount payable for
carrying large instruments like drums, bass fiddles, and harps to
and from the session).

The Phonograph Record Trust Agreement provides for the
payment of a percentage of record sales to the trust. This
money is used to fund free concerts and other performances by
union musicians at charitable and civic activities. The money is
distributed by the Musicians Performance Trust Fund to nonprofit grantees throughout the country, usually the local musicians unions, which use the money to pay musicians for their
performances at prevailing minimum wage scale rates.

The Phonograph Record Manufacturers Special Payments
Fund also provides for payment of a percentage of record sales,
as does the previous agreement. All the money collected by this
fund, minus administrative costs, is distributed to recording
musicians over a five-year period. That is, a musician who plays
on a recording session in 1980 will receive payments from this
fund from 1981 through 1986. The amount the musician receives
is calculated according to the ratio of the musician's total
wages for recording during a year to the total wages of *all*
musicians who recorded that year, payable on a sliding (diminishing) scale basis over the five years.

The three agreements mentioned above are interlocked. A
producer or company that is signatory to one will be a signatory to all of them.

Becoming a signatory to the agreements is frequently mis-construed as "getting a license to record." While signing the agreements is similar to being licensed in the sense that union musicians won't work for nonsigners, there's no piece of paper involved that's called a license.

A producer or company applies to the Phono Department of the AFM at 1500 Broadway, New York, N.Y. 10036, to become a signatory to the agreements. The AFM then forwards the application to the local union that covers the geographic area in which the producer or company operates. The executive board of the local union calls the applicant in for an interview to discuss the purposes for which the application is made, to determine the names and backgrounds of all the people in-volved in the recording venture, and to judge the financial capabilities of the applicant in the context of the applicant's ability to make all required payments of wages to the musi-cians, to taxing authorities, and to the trust and fund covered by the other agreements. If the local union is satisfied with the applicant's bona fides, the application will be approved and sent back to New York, which will then send copies of all three agreements to the applicant for signature.

There is no charge for entering into the agreements. How-ever, the applicant will be required to send a nonrefundable $100 (as of August 1979) to the Musician's Performance Trust Fund as a deposit against the amounts that may become due under the Phonograph Record Trust Agreement. This is the sum that is widely referred to incorrectly as the "fee" for the "license."

When the applicant receives copies of all the agreements, signed by the appropriate parties in New York (the union and the administrators of the other agreements), the producer or company is then free to hire union musicians for recording sessions in compliance with the terms and conditions of the Phonograph Record Labor Agreement.

The whole process of getting set up under the agreements takes from a few weeks to a few months, depending mainly on how frequently the executive board of the local union meets and how early it will schedule the interview with the applicant.

It is important to note that musicians are not required to work for minimum scale. Top sidemen and session players demand, and get, more than scale, or overscale.

PRODUCER CONTRACTS

When a producer is a member of the recording company, his or her services may be performed simply as an employee, and compensation may be paid or accrued on the books. Another alternative is that the producer's compensation may simply be accepted as the producer's contribution to the overall venture, as is often the case with young companies.

Outside producers, on the other hand, will expect to be paid. The compensation arrangement should be contained in an agreement with the producer.

A sample producer's contract is contained in *This Business of Music*, 1977 edition (Form 14, page 551). This agreement requires the producer to deliver finished master tapes to the company and establishes a production cost budget that the producer cannot exceed unless agreed to by the company or unless the producer pays for the overrun. The producer is required to produce a specified number of single sides— effectively the same as "cuts" in an album or other long-playing record—within the budgeted amount. The artists to be used on the sessions are specified by reference to the company's separate agreement with the artists.

The stock record production agreement provides for payment of the producer's services and expenses by means of royalties on records actually sold—excluding promotional give-away copies, bonus records, and certain other incentive records—at regular prices in the United States and for lower royalties on record club and foreign sales. The computation of the royalty amount is based on the nominal list price of the record, minus customary packaging charges—typically 15 percent of list price—multiplied by 90 percent of the records actually sold, multiplied by the agreed royalty rates applicable to the kind of sales involved (domestic, foreign, record club, for examples).

The royalty rates depend on whether the company found and signed the artists or they were brought to the company by the producer, and whether the company or the producer is obligated to pay the artist royalties. For many years, the basic royalty rate was 3 percent when the company named the artists and paid the artist royalties, but there are indications that hot producers are demanding, and getting, up to 4 percent at present. When the producer is obligated to pay the artists' royalties, the rate is increased to cover that expense and the total may run to 10 percent or more. An extraordinary case has been reported (*Fortune,* April 23, 1979) in which ex-Beatle Paul McCartney did a deal with CBS involving a 22 percent (combined artist and producer) rate.

Royalties are typically payable only after the company has recovered all of its production costs, even though the royalty may begin to be earned from the sale of the very first record. Whether royalties are earned from the point at which the company has recouped its production costs or are earned retroactively to first sales is a matter of negotiation between the producer and the company. The stock agreement contains alternate clauses to reflect whichever arrangement is made.

As a practical matter, producers are paid money up front in the form of advances against royalties. Few, if any, producers will work strictly on the contingency basis envisioned by royalties on sales, since the producer has no control over the company's marketing and promotional efforts, upon which royalty-generating sales are dependent. The advances are recoverable by the company from earned royalties; that is, actual payments to the producer begin only after the company has deducted advances from royalties earned.

There are advantages to both the producer and the company in royalty arrangements. The producer is obviously motivated to produce the best possible record within budget in order to reap the sizable rewards a hit can bring in the form of royalties. The company is able to defer some of the expenses of record production up to the point at which records have been manufactured, are being sold, and are producing income. A "name" producer, who might charge a flat fee in the tens of thousands of dollars to produce an album, may be induced to produce for little more in the way of advances than his or her out-of-pocket expenses. This will usually occur only when the producer is persuaded that the talent, the concept, the material, and the company's economic and marketing strengths are all strong enough to promise a very sizable sale and correspondingly large royalties.

Not all record producers are big names in the business. Around major recording areas like Los Angeles and Nashville, one can find free-lancers who produce thousands of demo records, first records, and specialty records for which there is no clear-cut certainty of volume sales. Such producers commonly produce records on a fixed-fee basis. Depending on how busy the producer is, his or her experience with specific kinds of music (e.g., country, jazz), and other factors, these fees range from about $100 to $500 per single side and from $500 to $2,500 for an album, without any royalty participation. Others work for an hourly rate, also without royalty participation, with typical fees in the $25-to-$75 range for time spent on the project.

It is beneficial to both the producer and the company to put the agreement between them into writing.

4

The Producer's Role

A record is the end product of an effort by a creative team. In addition to musicians, the team typically includes studio engineers, vocalists, arrangers, and copyists. The team leader is the producer.

There are several routes a person may take toward the role of producer.

Some producers enter the business by discovering and developing talent, formulating a concept for a record, and presenting a ready-to-record package to an existing label, which then manufactures, promotes, and distributes the end product.

A second route is similar with respect to the discovery and development of talent and concept formulation but involves people who create a new label to produce, manufacture, and market the records. People who become producers this way are often musicians bent on promoting their own talents or those of a group they have formed, or people who are outside the industry mainstream, such as doctors, lawyers, and businessmen who discover and invest in local talent for reasons that range from real economic motivation to ego trips.

Successful recording stars—often in company with associated professionals such as agents, personal managers, and promoters—frequently break away from the labels with which they originally signed to form their own production companies and/or labels and/or music publishing companies. The producer may be any of the people involved in such a venture.

Yet another kind of producer is the individual who has been a producer for a group or a label and has enjoyed such successes that he or she is sought out by either other artists or other labels to produce records on a nonexclusive basis. Deals made with these "hired guns" can cover from one record to several over a period of time. If the A&R (artist and repertoire) department of a label identifies potentially winning talent, it may want to bring in an outside big-name producer to help minimize the risks involved in launching new talent on records.

No matter how a person comes to fill the role of producer, the producer's responsibilities are the same: organization and management of the creative team to give birth to a recording that meets a predetermined set of artistic goals at affordable cost. To meet these challenges, a producer will at various times be tested as a sensitive and perceptive critic of musical art, as an engineer, as a businessman, as a diplomat, and as an arbitrator of conflict. But the producer's ultimate task is to serve as a *consumer advocate,* for the more accurately the producer's decisions reflect those that the buying public would make if it had the opportunity to vote on the many options of the production process the better the record's chance for success. The producer's ears and mind must be those of the audience that will eventually make or break the record with its purchasing decisions.

THE CONCEPT

Every record begins with a concept, and the more closely the concept that precedes any practical production work defines the ultimate end product, the better. Record concepts come from an almost unlimited range of sources. Current events inspired *Lots More Crude or No More Food*. Love, hate, and other emotions are at the root of countless record concepts. A new sound can be the basis of a record concept, as was the case in Ross Bagdasarian's "chipmunk" records, featuring the squeaky-voiced "Alvin."

The Mormon Tabernacle Choir Sings the Best of the Sex Pistols may be the epitome of poor concepts, but the title alone does give a substantial amount of definition to the end product, should anyone ever venture to produce it. It clearly identifies the artists (the choir) and the material that will be done (a selection from songs performed or previously recorded by the Sex Pistols). Because there are few recording studios large enough to accommodate the Mormon Tabernacle Choir, and because the travel costs involved in getting the choir to a studio would be huge, it's obviously better to obtain a portable recording van and do the basic recordings on location at the tabernacle itself. Even a couple of potential markets for the finished album are defined: Mormons of somewhat unusual taste and Sex Pistols fans who inadvertently mistake the Mormon Tabernacle Choir for a new punk rock group.

This concept, however, still needs fleshing out. Is the musical approach going to be to try to get punk rock sounds from the choir, or should it be to try somehow to give a religious feeling to Sex Pistols material? Should the product be one album or a multialbum set? What might the final jacket look like?

Whether the producer originates the concept or gets it from someone else, he or she should have as clear an idea as possible as to what the final record is going to be before starting production. This is important because the concept itself is going to define how the record will be produced, how long production will take, the facilities that will be needed and, in large measure, what production will cost. The concept will also provide some classification of the potential buying audience for the record: acid rock enthusiasts are not likely to buy too many traditional Dixieland albums, and conversely.

Titles help to define records, but the title isn't always the first thing that's thought about in developing a concept. More often, someone who is, or intends to become, a record producer hears a musical group and thinks, "Hey, they're good! They ought to be on a record!" Or a piece of material performed by a group may generate such enthusiasm in a live audience that the producer thinks the *material* ought to be recorded, either by the group that's performing it or by some other group the producer thinks might do it even better and more effectively. The most common inspiration for new recordings of new groups comes from the group itself. Typically, its members note its successes in getting and holding nightclub gigs and in receiving repeated inquiries about where its records are available, and decide to make a record. In an instant—not fully aware of the role being thrust upon him or her—the leader of the group becomes a potential record producer.

The initial statement of the concept in such a case might well be, "We'll do our ten best numbers on an album."

That simple statement may be very good. It effectively states that the material to be used is well rehearsed so that expensive studio time won't be wasted fixing "fluffs" in new tunes or arrangements. It suggests that the material to be done has received audience acclaim that will help to sell finished records. It may even suggest a title for the album: *The Best of . . . .*

So simple a statement may also lead to difficulties. A performing group that depends heavily on visuals—costumes, make-up, lighting effects, choreography—during live performance of its best material will probably have to alter that material substantially to make it effective as a sound recording. It might be better to consider different material in which such obstacles are not present.

In theory, the development of a concept ought to proceed wholly within the framework of art. In practice, records that sell often evolve artistically subject to technical and commercial considerations and limits.

The key technical limitation is the amount of time that can be recorded on one side of a disc. There is no way to cram a ten-minute-long concert number on one side of a 45 rpm single, and possibly not even on both sides. Whatever music is to be released in disc form will have to conform to the maximum time constraints discussed in Chapter 2.

A technical choice arises with respect to how the original recording is going to be done.

Direct-to-disc will result in records of the highest fidelity and lowest noise, but they demand perfect performance of a whole side of a record without interruption. There is no way to fix a performance error; if a fluff is serious enough to be considered ruinous to the performance, the whole side must be recorded again, perhaps many times, until it is right. This can have a serious impact on studio time required, and collaterally on studio costs. Moreover, the nature of the direct-to-disc manufacturing process and the associated quality control dictate that the number of records that can be made from a master is limited to a few thousand; this can be a major marketing consideration.

Recording directly on two-track tape provides some latitude to both performers and the producer. At worst, only one song at a time has to be performed perfectly, as differentiated from a whole side in direct-to-disc. There is some opportunity for fixes through careful editing. The fidelity of the manufactured recordings will be second only to direct-to-disc as a result of fewer generations in the process from live music to salable pressing. But direct-to-two-track recording demands a perfect job of engineering; the mix that is done during the live performance is the final mix. This is by no means impossible; in fact, that is precisely what every engineer was expected to do routinely before multitrack recording came along. Unfortunately, many younger engineers have never had to do a live mix, so a producer will want to check the experience credentials of any engineer assigned to attempt such an endeavor. Direct-to-two-track recording is a sensible and economical means and is capable of providing fine recordings, especially from smaller groups that use acoustical instrumentation.

Groups that are heavy in electronic augmentation or instruments, and which depend on the complicated effects and tricks that can be engineered into performances, are pretty much compelled to record multitrack. There is tremendous flexibility for both the performers and the producers to correct, modify, and enrich the performance through various processes. These include editing; dubbing; bouncing, which means transferring material from one recorded track to an empty track, adding effects or other premixed material in the process; and machine speed alteration. The penalty is that multitrack involves at least one additional generation in the path from performance to pressing, with resulting distortion, diminution of fidelity, or signal-to-noise ratio, or any combination of these. Multitrack recording involves the highest studio costs both because rates are higher for multitrack machine use and because of the time-consuming mixdown process associated with multitrack recording.

Digital recording, when it becomes widely available, will combine the noise and fidelity advantages of direct-to-two track, with the operational flexibility of multitrack at somewhat greater than multitrack cost. Some feel it will equal direct-to-disc in noise and fidelity advantages.

The commercial considerations that touch on concept come into play on several fronts.

The first of these is how much music to put on a record. This is not a major question with respect to a single, but it is where LP albums are concerned. More music means more time and cost for musicians and studio activities. Each additional song, regardless of length, will add to copyright royalty cost unless it is in the public domain. On the other hand, the consumer has to be considered. One noted producer, Bill Szymczyk of Bayshore Studios, remarks that anything less than seventeen minutes per side is cheating the customer (for a $7.98 LP). Review of about 150 albums indicates, however, that many producers and labels are influenced by the fact that thirty minutes of music (about fifteen minutes per side) is what is allowed under the Phonograph Record Labor Agreement for two basic recording sessions. Generally, smaller independent labels are more strongly influenced by this factor than the majors, and clerks at several record stores indicated that consumers are generally not highly conscious of total album time.

Two other commercial factors should be considered during concept development.

Rock and disco buyers have a clear liking for long cuts that hold a tempo or mood as they dance or indulge in other recreational activities. LP cuts that are longer than ten minutes are not unheard of. But radio stations that provide the air play that is so crucial to a record's initial exposure and ultimate success want far shorter cuts in the interests of programming variety, more facile scheduling, and insertion of revenue-producing commercials. A related factor is that older juke-boxes, many of which are still in service, cannot accept anything other than single records, so that any selections too long for single release will be denied exposure through these older machines.

Generally, length of cut is more important to AM radio broadcasters than to FM broadcasters. FM station pacing is typically slower, although this can be expected to change as the FM audience continues to grow (e.g., as more automobiles have FM receivers). During concept development, and in the ensuing preparation of arrangements and actual recording, a producer may want to make provisions for cutting an abbreviated version of any song with clear-cut hit potential so that the short version can be released as a single for promotional use on jukeboxes and radio stations.

The order in which selections are recorded on an LP is important. If the LP is a "standalone" record that is not associated with a single, the song with the greatest hit potential should be the first selection on side A and should be followed by the song with the second-highest hit potential. The third-best song should be the opener on side B. The next two best songs should become the final cuts on sides A and B respectively. It is important to open each side of an album with the best available material, because the cuts that radio disc jockeys are likely to play most are the first cuts, which are easier to cue on the turntable. The second easiest cut to cue on a record is the last one, which is why strong material should be used on the final cuts.

Producer Dave Pell notes that a hot-selling single is what propels an album to big sales. He feels that an existing single upon which an album is based should be the final selection on side A, the next potential single should be the opener on side A, the third potential single should be the opener on side B, a strong song should be the closer on side B, and the remaining songs should run in the order of strongest to weakest as the interior cuts on both sides.

Tunes in the same tempo or key should not be consecutive. If necessary, transpose into another key or change the tempo, or substitute an equally strong tune that fits these criteria. Of the rules for concept planning, this is the least stringent, however; it is better to have a tune follow in the same key or tempo—but definitely not both—than to abandon a good tune for a weaker one. Nor do you want to upset the best-balanced sequence achievable within the framework of the other rules of thumb.

The concept should also include a preliminary schedule. If a record is based on some current event, the record has to be done instantly. For example, someone might well have done a record on the events at Three Mile Island. And an album headed for a Christmas market has to be finished no later than August; earlier is even better. A record that requires the talents of a specific individual or group of individuals may have to be scheduled to take advantage of their availability in one place at the same time. A record that might be partially or wholly financed by a nightclub at which a group has a long engagement, with the financing being the price the club management pays in return for mention in the liner notes or title, should be produced as early in the engagement as possible.

A well-defined concept is the basis for planning and managing the successive steps of production and is the cornerstone upon which the vitally important advance budget is constructed. A thoroughly defined concept may also prove to be the key to getting outside financing for the record project.

A worksheet that may be used to help define the concept is shown in Figure 3. The proposed song sequence can be listed as 1-A, 2-B, to indicate the cut sequence on each side of the record. The purpose of each studio session, such as live recording or mixdown, should be indicated after the name of the studio. All the remaining listed items have a cost impact on the final record.

MUSIC PREPARATION

Some music—notably classical works and material to be done by large musical aggregations such as marching bands, choirs, show bands, and big bands—is formalized by a composer's score or arrangements. Music played by an organized group, whether originally written out or not, frequently gains the structure of a formalized score or arrangement through rehearsal and repeated performance. A great deal of jazz is played without anything having been written down except perhaps a few bars of an introduction, some riffs, and an ending.

Whether or not formal arrangements are required and whether or not the producer gets involved in the development of arrangements depends on the circumstances, the performers, and the material.

If a producer is working with an organized group, most of the purely musical decisions will have been made. The reason the group is being recorded is that it has a sound and a feel that someone has decided is marketable, and the producer's aim ought to be to preserve those characteristics in the recording.

The other extreme is the situation in which a producer is working with a new piece of material and has the job of presenting that material in the best way possible. In this case, the producer will conceive a desired sound, hire an arranger to write anything from a musical sketch to a full score, and pick the musicians who will do the material during the recording session.

Most of a producer's work is likely to fall between the

FIGURE 3
Concept Definition Form

CONCEPT DEFINITION

Proposed Title

ARTISTS
(List all required instrumentation and vocalists by name. Include sweetening personnel.)

SONGS

Title	Sequence	Time	Arrangement Required?	Public Domain?

TECHNICAL

Studios/Locations   Purpose

Record: ( ) Direct-to-disc   ( ) Two-track   ( ) Multitrack   ( ) 15IPS   ( ) 30IPS

GRAPHICS

		Front	Back
Original artwork to be:	From drawing, painting	( )	( )
	From photographs	( )	( )
	Line drawing or type	( )	( )
	Type only	( )	( )
	Full-color	( )	( )
	One- or Two-color	( )	( )

SCHEDULE

Task	*Completion Date*
Arrangements	
Live sessions	
Mixed-down master	

extremes of no control and total control over musical arrangements. From a producer's viewpoint, the more complete the arrangements are for the music to be recorded, the faster the session is likely to go. Within limits, complete charts give the producer the flexibility to replace a musician in case of illness, accident, or even ineptness, and to pick and choose among available players. Full charts also facilitate planning in terms of selection time and sequence and may be generated for just these purposes. Finally, completely scored music in the hands of good musicians virtually guarantees the reproduction of a desired sound. Even though the solo choruses cannot be duplicated exactly, there are quire a few bands that do a very creditable job with Glenn Miller, Dorsey, and similar arrangements, even though none of the original musicians are on the bands.

Most modern American music is structured to support one or more lead vocalists or instrumentalists in solo roles. It is rare that the solos are written, and there is a danger that spontaneity will be lost if they are. This is a producer's judgment call.

If arrangements are required, either the bandleader or the producer should have the work done by a professional arranger whose prior work with similar material has been successful and who is capable of writing to whatever presold sound and feel an organized group offers. In other words, don't call a Lawrence Welk chartist for an acid rock arrangement. Arranger's fee minimums are part of the Phonograph Recording Labor Agreement, as are fees for copyists, who take the parts for individual instruments off the conductor's score that the arranger will write.

The concept may contemplate the desirability of sweetening, in which additional musical performances augment the work of the originally recorded group. Sweetening occurs in several forms, including background vocals either as harmony lines or as rhythmic patterns under a lead vocal or instrumental solo, and instrumental backgrounds such as string-section chorus or counterpoint.

If a song is to be sweetened, this fact must be considered in planning the number of sessions required and the amount of studio time needed, and the various costs must be included in the production budget.

Tailoring tune durations to available record time is an important part of music preparation efforts. The total duration of the music *and* the silent time between consecutive cuts of an album (six to eight seconds) should be within the engineering time limitations discussed earlier. Another item that may be considered is restriction of individual tunes to less than 5.5 minutes in length to prevent an increase in the copyright royalty. In addition, consideration should be given to limiting the total music content of an album to 30 minutes, the amount usable from two basic recording sessions under the union labor agreement.

If the music is fully arranged, the only control over selection time is to modify the tempo. There is relatively little room for tempo variation without impairing the feel of a tune, but a "stretch" or "shrink" of two or three percent (five to seven seconds in a nominal four-minute tune) is often possible. The other option is to alter the arrangement length; for example, a repeat can be made from the bridge instead of from the top of a chorus, or a chorus, intro, tag, or segue can be cut or added.

A computer program that is designed for use with a Hewlett Packard HP-97 programmable calculator is furnished in Appendix A. This program greatly simplifies timing calculations for producers, arrangers, and leaders. The number of beats per measure and the number of measures in a full chorus of the song must be known. After these data are keyed in, the program will calculate total number of choruses, tempo (beats per minute), and total time when any two of these factors are known. For example, if the tune is in 4/4 time and is thirty-two bars long, and it is desired to play 5 full choruses at 120 beats per minute, the program will calculate the total tune time of five minutes and twenty seconds. This duration will not fit on a 45 rpm single, so the question is, "What will?" Reentering data of 4 beats per measure, thirty-two bars per chorus, and 120 beats per minute, but entering four minutes (the time limit on a 45) instead of 5 choruses, the program will calculate that 3 choruses plus twenty-four bars can be played in four minutes.

The tune might easily be rearranged to provide for an eight-bar introduction, 2 full choruses, a four-bar segue or modulation to another key, another full chorus, and an eight-bar tag (ending). The tune now has a total of 3 choruses and twenty bars, which equals 3⅝ or 3.625 choruses. The program will calculate three minutes and fifty-two seconds of time, which is neatly within the limitation of a 45 rpm single.

Suppose the same tune was to have been an album cut six choruses long. The time would run to six minutes and twenty-four seconds. By replanning for five choruses, the duration of five minutes and twenty seconds will save five cents per album in copyright fees—enough to operate a fairly large yacht for a day if a million copies are sold.

Timing calculations can be done with an ordinary calculator or by hand, using the equations below. In these equations, playing time has to be expressed in decimal minutes rather than as minutes and seconds. To convert minutes and seconds into decimal minutes, simply drop the minutes, divide the remaining seconds by 60, then add the minutes to the answer. Thus, 3 minutes and 45 seconds equals 45/60 = 0.75 plus 3 = 3.75 decimal minutes. To reconvert from decimal minutes back to minutes and seconds, drop the minutes, multiply the decimal fraction (to the right of the decimal point) by 60 and re-add the minutes.

$$\text{Total playing time} = \frac{\text{Beats per measure} \times \text{measures to be played}}{\text{Metronome setting}}$$

$$\text{Measures to be played} = \frac{\text{Playing time} \times \text{metronome setting}}{\text{Beats per measure}}$$

$$\text{Metronome setting} = \frac{\text{Beats per measure} \times \text{measures to be played}}{\text{Playing time}}$$

A metronome is required at the studio so that the preplanned tempos can be duplicated during sessions. Some studios have electronic metronomes connected to the mixing console so that the beat can be sent to performers' headphones at the start of a tune, or even all the way through if the rhythm section has any tendency to race or drag. The metronome beat can also be recorded on an unused track of a multichannel recording to serve as a "click track" for performers who add tracks after the basic tracks are laid; for example, vocals and sweetening. The metronome beat does not record on the live music tracks and is not heard in final master tapes.

REHEARSALS

Any music that is going to be recorded should be rehearsed thoroughly before the studio sessions. During the rehearsals the producer should carefully time every song and use a metronome to set or determine the actual tempo so that the tempo can be duplicated later in the studio sessions, thus ensuring that the tunes come in at the preplanned durations.

The goal of rehearsals should be to get the musical performances nailed down well enough so that repeat performances in the studio are intended to fix "fluffs" rather than to try out new ideas or concepts. A studio is an expensive rehearsal hall.

An exception to the foregoing may occur with respect to some modern music in which the producer and the engineer will attempt special electronic effects during the session rather than later during mixdown.

Small organized groups will generally rehearse on their own time and without cost to the production. Musicians and groups hired specifically for a recording session will probably have to be paid to rehearse, and a rehearsal contract should be filed with the local union.

If the music is going to be performed from complete arrangements, the producer should obtain copies of the scores for each tune. If the music is going to be done with "head arrangements," or from sketchy charts, the producer should note the structure of each tune, including chorus-by-chorus listings of ensemble and solo choruses and cues for unusually loud or soft passages and highlight effects, such as the use of a chime. From the scores and/or notes, the producer can make guide sheets that will be used in the control room during the recording session.

CHORUS GUIDE SHEETS

During recording sessions the studio engineer on the mixing console, or board, simply adjusts volume levels (gains) for maximum signal from each microphone or instrument channel, short of distortion, when recording multitrack. On direct-to-disc and two-track sessions, however, the engineer is doing a live mix and is striving for the total balance that will be heard on the final record by the consumer. To do this effectively, the engineer needs to know just what is going to happen during each selection. As the solo line or lead passes from one instrumentalist to another, or to a vocal group, or to the entire group in ensemble, the engineer has to make adjustments to individual channel gains to preserve the desired balance and, commonly, to cut the gain on channels not momentarily in use to preserve best signal-to-noise characteristics in the recording.

A good mix can be achieved much more quickly if the engineer reads music and is provided with a conductor's score or a chorus guide similar to that shown in Figure 4 for each tune. For the song "Sunday," for example, the engineer would set the initial balance on the ensemble. At the end of the first chorus, he or she would probably fade down the gains on the clarinet and trombone channels during the trumpet solo, increasing them again during the riff under the bridge, then fading them again on the last eight bars of the chorus. Similarly, just before the end of the first chorus, he or she would begin to bring the piano level up slightly for the piano solo in the second chorus, and so on. The guide is just a road map that gives the engineer the opportunity to anticipate needed gain changes so that they can be executed smoothly and so unobtrusively that they are not obvious to the listener. Guides serve the same purpose in multitrack mixdown.

FIGURE 4
Typical Chorus Guide Sheet

SONG TITLE ___"SUNDAY"___

KEY OF _C_   TEMPO: ___150___   PROJECTED TIME ___3:50___

CHORUS	BARS	PLAYED BY	REMARKS
INTRO	8	ENSEMBLE	
#1	32	ENSEMBLE	
#2	16	TRUMPET SOLO	ENSEMBLE ORGA.
	8	BRIDGE-TPT. SOLO	CHORDS UNDER
	8	TRUMPET SOLO	
#3	16	PIANO SOLO	TO BRIDGE
	8	CLARINET SOLO	
	8	PIANO	
#4	16	TROMBONE	TO BRIDGE
	8	TENOR	ENSEM. LAST 2 BA. OF BRIDGE
	8	ENSEMBLE	
TAG	4	DRUM BREAK	
	4	ENSEMBLE OUT	

RECORDING SESSION CONTRACTS

Record companies that are signatories to the Phonograph Record Labor Agreement are required to notify the local AFM union in whose jurisdiction the recording will be done before beginning any sessions. Most locals require at least twenty-four hours' advance notice. Some, notably Los Angeles Local 47, have highly formalized procedures and requirements, including the requirement for new record companies that a bond be furnished that is sufficient to assure that the musicians will be paid.

In addition, the company will also be required to enter into a contract with the musicians, which defines time, place, and hours of the session and the amounts payable to the players and to the AFM-EPW Fund. These contracts—one for each session—are prepared on the AFM's Form B by the company, the bandleader, or the contractor and are executed by the company and the bandleader. The contracts are filed with the local union, which sends appropriate copies to the AFM's National Contracts Division in New York.

Similar contracts are required when the company hires vocalists who are AFTRA members.

These contracts with musicians and vocalists are separate from and supplements to a company's agreement under the AFM Phonograph Record Labor Agreement and the AFTRA Code. The PRLA and the Code are basic to all recording sessions, while these contracts deal with specific sessions. The producer may not actually be the person to sign on behalf of the company, but should take responsibility for ensuring that the contracts are correctly and timely prepared, that they reflect the understanding with the musicians, and that they are filed with the proper unions.

USE OF CONTRACTORS

Under the AFM-PRLA and the AFTRA Code, a contractor is required to be hired on sessions involving twelve or more instrumental sidemen or more than two vocalists. Usually, the contractor will be one of the sidemen or vocalists.

A contractor can be very helpful to a producer. The contractor will help locate musicians needed for a session, gather Social Security and other data needed to prepare contracts, may actually prepare the contract forms, and will generally serve as a coordinator to ensure that performers are aware of session schedules and locations and what instruments they will be expected to bring to the sessions. In the major recording areas—Los Angeles, New York, etc.—the contractors themselves tend to be top-caliber musicians who have extensive knowledge of the local scene, of who's available and what their skills are, so that an out-of-town producer, especially, can benefit from the addition of a contractor even on sessions for which a contractor is not otherwise required.

STUDIO SELECTION

The choice of a studio or studios is based on several factors, including facilities and equipment available, acoustics, personnel, location, prices, and reputation. Virtually any modern studio can turn out good recordings, but excellent recordings demand a fairly good match among requirements defined by the concept and the actual hardware, room(s), and people a studio can offer to translate the concept into a finished master disc or tape.

If the concept calls for direct-to-disc recording, the studio must have a recording lathe. For all other approaches, the recording equipment will be tape recorders.

If the decision is made to record multitrack, the next decision that must be made is how many tracks the recording machine should have: eight, twelve, twenty-four, or more. The answer is not quite as simple as one track per instrument, although that was the way multitrack recording started. Pianos are often double-miked, with one mike ultimately being assigned to the left channel and the other to the right channel of the final two-track master tape. Drum sets are generally miked with three to six microphones, depending on the complexity of the set. But if a limited number of recording tracks are available, several of these mikes may be premixed into one or two tape tracks. Acoustic guitars are typically recorded with a microphone feeding one track on the recorder and the internal pickup feeding another, the miked channel providing ambiance and fingerboard sounds that the producer may want to hear. Sweetening and vocals can occupy more channels and recorded tracks, and a producer may want to use tracks not used for live recording to bounce music from one live-recorded track to an empty track as effects (e.g., echo) are added. The track processed in this way then becomes the track that will be used in mixdown.

All engineers and many producers want to record every conceivable combination of sounds in every conceivable way to allow the greatest freedom of choice in mixdown. One school of thought says that the higher cost of studio time for use of the larger machines is worthwhile because it affords this flexibility. Another school of thought states that using a 40-track recorder to produce a record from a seven- or eight-piece group indicates a serious lack of preplanning, discipline, or talent on the part of the producer and/or the engineering team. Multimillion-album sellers have come from members of both schools. What is certain is that the more tracks that are available on the recorder, the longer and more expensive the mixdown process will become. Whether audience-perceptible (selling) differences result from ultraelaborate recording, processing, and remix efforts is not as clear.

Some studios are equipped with automated mixdown facilities. After all the live tracks have been laid, the producer works with the engineer to adjust the level (gain) controls on all channels to produce the desired end balance on the master tape. As a song progresses, channel gains are raised and lowered to highlight or accentuate performance sound. These control moves, some of which can occur in rapid sequence—perhaps more rapid than the engineer can handle with only two hands— are recorded in the form of digital control signals on the original tape. When the tape is played back, each channel gain control follows the preprogrammed moves—not physically, but through electronic duplication of the original physical moves. If the producer is not satisfied with the trial mix, the tape can be played back again and the producer can change levels on individual channels without disturbing the mix on other channels. The modified moves are written over the original control moves and then become the operative control signals. The process of replaying the original tape and inserting corrective control moves continues until a point is reached at which the mix is precisely what the producer wanted when the original tape is played all the way through. At that point the tape is played back once more while the two-track master is recorded. There is the prospect that the extra generations involved in multitrack recording may be reduced through the use of automated boards; once the final mix is programmed into the computer, the master disc can be cut directly from the multitrack machine without the need for an intermediate two-track tape.

In and of itself, automated mixdown does not make better records. It can reduce necessary mixdown time because it relieves the producer of the concern that the engineer cannot or will not follow a desired set of control moves. As trial mixes are played back, the producer can devote full attention to the sound instead of dividing attention between the sound and the control console.

If a producer has specific preferences as to the types of microphones that should be used to record various voices and instruments, the studio's ability to provide those mikes may become a selection factor. But unless there are compelling reasons why a producer has such preferences, the engineer should be given as much latitude as possible to pick and use the mikes with which he or she is familiar, and which the engineer has used successfully on other sessions of a similar nature.

Every modern studio has one or more echo, or reverb, options—an acoustical echo chamber, an AKG echo plate, digital delay, or some other mechanisms. Every echo method produces a different texture, and this may influence studio selection. New producers should probably pick a studio with a live chamber, which is rare, or one that has an AKG plate, since these echo systems are widely considered to be best. New producers are also cautioned against the excessive use of echo, a flaw that afflicts too many first records.

Today all studios also have one or more facilities for noise reduction and/or compression and/or limiting. All of these devices are intended to help the engineer optimize the signal-to-noise ratio of the recorded tape.

Limiters and compressors either cut and "dump" signal levels above a certain predetermined level (limiting) or reduce the gain of a channel if average or peak (selectable) signal levels rise beyond a preset limit (compression). The purpose of limiting and compression is to prevent tape overload or saturation and the resulting distortion.

Noise reduction systems, such as Dolby™, operate in recording-like compressors and in playback-like expanders, which restore original signal levels by increasing channel gain on channels where and when gain had been reduced in recording. The noise reduction systems do this in discrete frequency bands—for example, bass, midrange, and treble—so that the signal energy in each of these sub-bands within the total audio spectrum is processed separately, without relationship to the energy in the other sub-bands.

The musical characteristics of signals in each channel can be modified by the equalizers, which act essentially like the tone controls on a high fidelity system.

From a producer's viewpoint, the thing to remember is that all of the engineer's hardware does something to alter the performance that is taking place on the other side of the glass. While the manipulation of the controls is the engineer's bailiwick, the producer must exercise the final judgment as to the choice and degree of use. Generally, the more limiting, compression, and EQ (*eek,* for equalization), the less pure the recorded sound. The question the producer has to answer is whether purity or impurity will sell the ultimate product. Then the producer must work with the engineer to achieve the results dictated by that answer.

Since the piano is essential to so much music, most studios have very high-quality grands or baby grands, and these are usually meticulously maintained and perfectly satisfactory for most keyboard players. Rarely, a studio may have to be selected on the basis of its ownership of a Steinway or Bösendorfer grand; some classical pianists simply won't play what they consider to be lesser instruments.

More and more studios have other instruments. They make these available either as an inducement to record at the studio or on a rental basis. They usually include, but are not limited to, electronic organs; Arp or Moog synthesizers; Fender-Rhodes, R.M.I., Yamaha, and other electronic keyboards, including clavinettes; harpsichords; celestes; and drum sets. The availability of these house instruments is more than a matter of mere convenience: their presence may save a sizable amount of money for cartage and cut down setup time as well. Of more importance is the fact that the studio that owns these instruments will usually offer some excellent techniques for recording them. Still, a producer should leave the final decision on using house instruments to the instrumentalists and should be aware of the need for any such instruments when considering prospective studios.

The kind of acoustics a studio's rooms—performance rooms, as differentiated from the control room—should have depends on the way the recording is to be done. For dry tracks, the room should be acoustically dead and should be large enough to allow physical separation of at least five feet between instruments miked live. Instruments feeding the board through direct boxes, with no acoustical output in the room save through headphones, can be placed anywhere. All performers have to have eye contact with all others. Portable baffles will be placed between any stand-up bass and other live instrument mikes, and the drum setup will be in a heavily baffled drum box. An acoustical piano will also be baffled or shrouded. Performers will largely hear each other and their own performances through headphones fed from the board. The goal of dry track recording is maximum isolation between instruments so that the track for any given instrument has as little crosstalk from any other instrument as possible.

If the objective is a more live sound, with presence, ambience, and a feeling of acoustical rather than engineered stereo, then the room itself must be more lively. It may not have a larger floor, but the ceiling is likely to be ten feet high or more and will have a somewhat reverberant feel instead of a feeling of total deadness. A live room is required for most direct-to-disc and direct-to-two-track work and is particularly desirable for big band and jazz recording in which the instrumentation is predominantly acoustical. Many studios have both live and dead rooms. Generally, artificial echo or reverb is a poor substitute for natural room reverberation. Material or groups that require a live room should not be recorded in a dead room, and vice versa.

In larger metropolitan areas, a producer should have little difficulty in finding several studios that can meet the technical requirements for a given production, and competition may result in a spread of prices for studios of similar capabilities. In this situation, the choice of the studio ought to be based on the engineering talent the studio can offer the production.

There are engineers who have done many rock and disco sessions that require dry tracks and great skill in such techniques as multiple-recorder flanging, "punch in" overdubbing, precision mechanical editing, and gimmicks such as pitch or tempo alteration with variable-speed machines and other devices. These engineers are savvy in miking rhythm sections to get the intense sound that is desired in much contemporary music and in the use of—even invention of—special-effect sounds that can be created by such methods as running the tape backward.

Other engineers are experienced in doing live mike work in live rooms and in the critical art of live mixing. These engineers are knowledgeable about acoustics, band layout within a studio, and mike selection and placement, and the kind of sound they get is often heard in fine jazz, pop, and classical recordings.

A producer should go to some pains to get an engineer who is attuned to and experienced with the kind of recording the producer has in mind. Listening to records that candidate studios have recorded, and comparing these recordings with others that reflect the producer's idea of the best engineering for similar groups and material, may help narrow the focus.

A producer can learn a great deal about candidate studios and engineers by talking with other producers. Accolades from other producers don't necessarily mean that a studio is right for a given session, and knocks may simply be the result of personality conflicts. But a producer who takes the time to investigate the experiences others have had with a given studio is somewhat more likely to achieve the overall objectives of the planned production than the producer who accepts studio promotional hyperbole at face value.

If possible, a producer should name two or three studios at which the session work might be done and then leave the negotiations and preparation of purchase orders to people on the business side of the organization.

ENGINEERING BRIEFING

Before the beginning of any session work, the producer should meet with the engineer(s) who will be doing the sessions to discuss the objectives of the session and to exchange views on needs, ideas, and approaches.

The engineer needs to know what instrumentation will be used on a session. This will generally lead to discussion of microphone selection and/or choices on the use of direct boxes. Plans for lead and background vocals should be discussed, and decisions should be made on which materials will be recorded live and which will be added in later tracking or sweetening sessions.

If the objective is a largely free, relatively unstructured and spontaneous performance by a self-contained jazz group, the engineer needs to know that this won't come about if the musicians are scattered all over the studio and are forced to wear headphones as they perform. The stereo separation that is commonly the engineer's goal may have to be sacrificed to allow the musicians to cluster together enough to "feel" each other's performance.

If, on the other hand, the secret to the whole planned record concept is in special effects that are going to be added in postsession recording and mixdown, the producer may want the tape engineered with dry tracks. This means that there will be maximum separation between instruments and that each instrument will be recorded on a multitrack recorder at the maximum level that the tape will accommodate, so as to obtain the best possible signal-to-noise and interchannel crosstalk ratios for the subsequent mixdown efforts.

The producer and engineer should talk through the music to be performed, working with the score or the guide sheet. The more the engineer knows about what's coming in the performance, the better the engineering is likely to be. A decision must be made as to whether the players of amplified instruments will make their own gain (volume control) adjustments or whether all level adjustments will be made on the board by the engineer. Board control is best, but it may be necessary to secure the gain controls in position with masking tape on instruments to prevent the player from making the moves that would be made instinctively in live performances.

The communication between a producer and an engineer is necessarily something of a mixture of art and engineering. If it is possible for the producer to convey the idea of a record and of the desired sound by reference to previously recorded materials, the engineer may be able to "reverse engineer" into the technique that was used to create those sounds in the first place. Today most engineers can listen to the sound of an instrument and get a pretty good idea of how the sound was achieved—for example, by flanging or hard-limiting (fuzzing), tape-speed change, and the like. But the producer has to be able to describe or provide an earlier recorded example of what he or she is after.

The producer should seriously consider having a work-print

cassette or reel-to-reel tape made of all live session recording. The term *work print* comes from the movie business, where a film print that is not color corrected or light balanced is used to do a first cut, or edit, on a film production. A work-print tape is one that contains the music with the studio monitor mix. The tape poses no threat to the studio, since it will be recorded on amateur equipment in an amateur format and the mix will seldom be anything like the final mix, but the tapes are very valuable to the producer. At the end of a day's recording, the producer can take these tapes home or to some other nonpressure environment and listen to them to detect unstable rhythms, bad notes, particularly desirable licks, and other aspects of the performed work. The producer can then use this information to plan next-day session work, to identify the need for retakes, and to determine when no further work on a given tune is necessary. The work print will also give the producer a feel for the possibilities for editing in the final edit and mixdown sessions.

SESSION DIRECTION

When the producer arrives at the studio for the session, the studio should be ready. If the piano is to be used, it should be tuned afresh. The engineers should have placed stools and microphones in approximate final positions. Headphones, if they are to be used by the performers during the session, should be connected and available at each performer's position. Tape machines should be loaded. The engineers should have completed all preliminary audio level setups and recorded a complete set of reference tones on the tape in accordance with preliminary engineer-to-engineer discussions with the mastering laboratory on lab requirements. This is very important when noise reduction systems such as Dolby™ and DBX™ are used during recording, as they are in most contemporary work.

When the performers arrive at the studio, the engineers will place them, connect-up to any instruments that are to be recorded direct (that is, by making an electrical connection to

the instrument or its amplifier speakers), and position microphones.

During rehearsals and the engineering briefing, the producer,
the engineer, and the musicians will make a decision as to
whether individual musicians will adjust the volume and/or
special effects (e.g., fuzzer, flanger) controls on amplified
instruments or whether all controls will be left at constant
settings, with level settings done by the engineer in the control
room on the mixing board. Either approach can be correct,
depending on the circumstances, and it is always easier for
musicians to do in the studio what they have done in live
performances. But whatever the decision, this is the time for
the producer to remind the players what it is.

With everything ready in the sound studio, the producer
joins the engineer at the mixing console and, using the talk-
back intercom between the control room and the studio, asks
the leader of the group to run through the first number. As the
tune is being run down, the engineer will make level, equalization, and possibly echo and other effect adjustments. If the
recording is being done direct-to-disc or on two-track tape, the
engineer will also adjust the pan pots (panoramic potentiome-
ters) to assign each instrument electronically to the spatial left,
center, or right of the release stereo recording. The tune may
have to be run through two or three times before the engineer
is satisfied with the mix.

At this point, if the recording is being made multitrack, what
the producer hears out of the monitor speakers is not necessarily a good mix, nor need it be. In multitrack, where each
instrument is recorded on its own tape channel, the engineering
objective is to achieve maximum recorded level on each channel without distortion. The producer should not be concerned
with the engineer's setup efforts. Rather the producer should be
very much concerned with, and should listen very closely to,
the sounds of the individual instruments. When the engineer has
finished with the setup, *then* the producer can and should voice
any questions and comments. If the producer wants to hear
fingerboard sounds from the guitar but can't, or if the balance

between the bass and treble ends of the piano seems uneven, or if the kick drum lacks an expected punch, the producer should tell the engineer, who will then make microphone, equalization, or other adjustments until the desired sound is achieved within the obvious limits of musicianship and studio facility capability.

The producer and engineer need to be able to communicate with each other. The producer has the ultimate responsibility for deciding what is and what is not good sound, but it is the engineer's responsibility to determine how to accomplish what is desired. A producer who persistently orders changes in equalization ("Bump up the 10 kHz EQ on the ride cymbal") instead of stating what he or she is after ("The ride cymbal needs to be a little brighter") will soon find himself or herself engineering rather than producing the record. Technical direction from the producer to the engineer—on matters such as choice of microphones, placement, equalization, limiting, and the like—should come only as a last resort after diplomatic suggestions and questions that hint at the desired answer have failed.

If the recording is being done direct-to-disc or on two-track tape, the mix the producer hears in the control room is exactly what the ultimate record buyer is going to hear. Now the producer has to be concerned not only with the sounds of individual instruments, but with the blend and their spatial positioning on the left and right channel monitor speakers. The engineer will be doing a live mix, adjusting gains on the various instrument channels in response to the flow of the music through ensemble, solos, and section (reeds, trumpets, etc.) parts.

Once the engineer and the producer agree on the technical elements, it is time to go for a take. The producer will advise the group over the talk-back. The leader or an assistant producer in the sound studio will turn on a metronome that has been preset to the desired tempo, then turn it off when the leader has the beat. The engineer will roll the tape and "slate" it (another term taken from the movie business) by recording the title of the tune and "Take One" from the microphone on the board. The leader counts off the beat and the session is under way. The producer will start the stopwatch, which is usually digital and console-mounted, on the first note of the tune.

As the song progresses, the producer should be completely dedicated to the role of critical appraiser on behalf of the ultimate consumer. Eyes closed to block out all visual distractions, the producer listens; the objects of his attention are missed notes, wrong notes, creeping tempo, extraneous sounds—coughing, rustling of paper as chart pages are turned—and, generally, the quality of the performance.

At the end of the first take, the performing group is going to want to hear what was recorded. The producer should announce that the tune will be played back to them in the studio; otherwise, the whole group will suddenly be in the control room. During the playback the producer again listens critically and makes notes. The replay also gives the producer the opportunity to double-check the stopwatch timing of the tune.

Following the replay, the producer should enter the studio and ask, "How did it sound?" If there have been fluffs or imperfections, the chances are very good that the performers will pick them up themselves so that the producer can either avoid criticizing or be able to limit suggestions for improvement to points the musicians did not pick up. The producer should particularly praise any highlights of the performance, remembering that even the toughest musicians are sensitive artists who can use all the inspiration and motivation they can get.

If there is unanimous agreement that the first take was satisfactory, move on to the next tune. If take one was less than perfect, do a second take and a third if needed. Although all the musicians will want to hear every take, remember that studio and musician costs continue during these playbacks. It is worthwhile, however, to play back part or all of a take if the playback can be accompanied by specific remedial suggestions or constructive criticism.

If a tune has not jelled in three takes, or four at most, then it is probably best to move on to the next tune and return to the first tune later. It is good practice to limit each tune after the first to two takes until all the tunes that are to be recorded have been done at least once, reserving improvement, refinement, and corrective takes on songs until after at least one full version of the album is in the can.

A good general instruction to the recording musicians is that if there is a serious fluff or bubble, such as a really bad note or failure of a soloist to come in on cue, the tune can be stopped in mid-performance by the leader or any player. If a fluff is minor, the musicians should ignore it and keep playing; the producer can decide whether it is a problem that can be fixed in the mix, tolerated in the released record, or is serious enough in his judgment to cut the take short. An engineer should be permitted to cut a take short for a pure engineering problem, but *never* for artistic reasons.

A musical group can be just like a football team in the sense that there will be some days on which everybody performs flawlessly and others on which the game is a shambles of fumbles, interceptions, and penalties or their musical equivalents. But while the football coach has to play out the game, come what may, the producer has the option of terminating a session early and rescheduling it for a later time at which everything will turn out to be psychologically, biorhythmically, astrologically, and musically better—or even perfect. The decision to cut short and reschedule a session may be expensive but nonetheless necessary to achieve the ultimate objective of market acceptability for the record.

It is partly to avoid the pitfalls involved in having a large group of people working together in perfect harmony that quite a lot of modern music is recorded in segments. It is not uncommon for a producer to lay down the rhythm tracks for all the songs on an album by calling in a keyboard player, a bass player, and one or more percussionists who will record only the rhythm patterns and possibly reference sketches of the melodic lines that may not even be used in the final recording of the

songs. In successive sessions, instrumental soloists, vocal soloists, ensemble vocals, or instrumental sweetening—even sound
effects—may be added to the multitrack master tape. During
each of the successive sessions the new players listen to the
previously recorded tracks through headphones and play their
parts in synchronization. To a degree the producer works
almost one-on-one with the series of performers and, in theory,
should be able to get optimum individual performances from
everyone. In practice, the feeling of such producer-conducted
music tends to be sterile and without warmth, but there is no
denying that it can also result in a very slick, professionally
packaged, highly marketable product.

It should be apparent that the foregoing technique is only
possible with multitrack but that it also affords additional
freedom to the producer with respect to artist selection and
scheduling. It is fairly common these days for rhythm tracks to
be laid down by a coterie of highly talented players in Muscle
Shoals, Alabama, on master tapes that will be completed in
Nashville, Los Angeles, New York, or Montserrat. The other
considerations are that the producer will have to supervise all
of the sessions, may have to travel extensively, and may be
committed to weeks of work on a single album.

A basic part of the producer's responsibility is to decide how
a recording is going to be produced and what sessions will be
needed to achieve the required end results.

One of the most difficult decisions a producer has to face is
that of determining when the recording work is *finished*. It is
perfectly normal for musicians to want to play every note and
every phrase to absolute perfection. The producer, as well,
should want the production to reflect the uncompromised
epitome of his or her skills. But if a record is to have any hope
of being an economic success, the producer will acknowledge,
accept, and manage sessions to completion within the confines
of the production budget. There must come a time at which the
producer calls a halt to repeated takes and declares each song
finished, no matter how much either the producer or any or all
of the musicians might want one last shot at improvement or

refinement. What makes this decision so difficult is that in the final analysis no one—neither the producer nor the musicians—can know with absolute certainty what is right and perfect from the viewpoint of the ultimate listening public. At best, the decision rests on a subjective guess today as to what will arouse and excite the sleeping giant tomorrow.

There is one situation in which a producer does not face that difficult decision. If the recording is being made of a live concert, the die is cast by the quality of that live performance.

During recording sessions a producer works with creative people, including engineers, who are very likely to have lots of suggestions. They may also undergo performance peaks and slumps; they may be taciturn or furiously temperamental; and they can be as physically and emotionally drained by the recording experience as if they had competed in an Olympic event. The producer has to be the stabilizer, the motivator, the critic, and the spiritual leader. But the producer must also be a firm, fair, decisive manager.

Since every creative situation differs from all others, there are no cut-and-dried rules to guide a producer's relationships with the people who are making the music. However, the following may be helpful.

It is usually worthwhile to listen to suggestions but not to encourage changes in the script or to depart from the pre-planned concept, which was developed without the immediate pressures that exist in the studio, unless the suggested improvement is so significant and valid that it would be foolish to ignore it.

Five hours is as long as any session should run, and it's generally better to hold them to four or less. The longer a session runs, the more likely it is that performance errors will increase and that the musical ideas of ad lib soloists will lose their spark. Long overtime sessions are also expensive.

Producers should be aware of a phenomenon that seems to be fairly common when retakes on a tune become necessary. A performance pattern shaped like an inverted bell tends to occur in which, after three or four takes, the quality goes down, bottoms out, and then starts back up. There are several options in this situation: keep playing away on the same tune, go to another tune for a while, take a break, or drop the tune for the rest of the session and start with it on the next session. None of these approaches is universally right, and the producer will have to make a choice based on familiarity with the players, the importance of perfection required for that specific tune in the scheme of a whole album, the amount of time left in the session, and, inevitably, budgetary considerations. The author has heard of but fortunately never experienced sessions in which more than forty takes have been required to get through the bell curve.

It is usually a good idea to let the musicians in a recording group waste a few minutes doing a tune that is not on the preplanned recording list. Whatever they pick will generally be a consensus tune with which all feel comfortable. When spontaneously performed, it just may turn out to be exceptional. Having an extra tune in the can can be a boon if one preplanned tune simply doesn't come off. It might even prove to be the start of a later album. At worst, it provides a brief respite from the pressure and discipline of the main session that can help to recharge the musical batteries. The engineer won't have a chorus guide sheet for such a free-form tune, but if it occurs in mid-session, the engineer will probably have enough experience with the group's sound to wing an adequate mix.

Union rules require breaks during recording sessions. If the musicians are psyched up and are on a roll, it's smarter to break the rule and continue than to interrupt and lose the winning performance. As a practical matter, the musicians are likely to feel the same way and won't raise the issue with the union as long as the producer is fair and does not attempt to extract more playing time than has been contracted for. The union requirements are contained in the Phonograph Record Labor Agreement.

MIXDOWN AND EDITING

When a multitrack master tape has been recorded correctly,

the producer has almost total command over what will be the final sound of the record. Except for a few premixed tracks—that is, a single recorded track onto which several instruments might have been recorded simultaneously, typically drums or sweetening—the producer can control the blend, highlighting, and postrecording equalization and echo on every individual instrument. During the recording, each track was recorded with maximum undistorted volume, and the crosstalk was minimized by acoustical or electrical isolation techniques the engineer used.

In "going for the mix," the four, eight, sixteen, twenty-four, thirty-two, forty or more tracks (possible when multiple multi-track recorders are used in synchronization) will all come down to two-track stereo. The producer now does exactly what he or she would have done in conjunction with the engineer if the recording had originally been made live, direct-to-disc, or on a two-track master. He or she positions the various instruments spatially by setting the pan pot for each channel so that the signal is routed to the left speaker, to the right speaker, or divided to favor left, right, or center, with center being equal division of the signal between the left and right speakers.

The producer will listen carefully to all the takes on a tune. If the best take was take three, except for some aberration that did not exist in takes one and two, the producer and the engineer might physically cut out the defect in take three and splice in the good material from take one or two, whichever was better. Alternatively, if the defect in take three involved a flaw in only one music track, the producer could opt simply to fade out that track completely during the faulty section or erase it and record the acceptable material from one of the other takes of the same music track onto the now vacant track in take three. The use of these physical and electronic editing techniques requires a nearly perfect match in key and tempo, which is another advantage of building on prerecorded rhythm tracks. An imperfect match is not necessarily fatal, however, since even individual performances can be corrected by rerecording the faulty track onto another tape, speed and time correcting that tape, then rerecording the correct material into the appropriate track of the master.

As a last resort the producer can call back the musician who played the faulty track, or even some other player of the same instrument, and rerecord the passage on the original master tape. This is an expensive solution and is seldom necessary if the producer has saved all the good takes that were recorded, as differentiated from recording over takes that are incomplete or not wholly satisfactory in the interest of conserving tape.

Once the best possible multitrack master has been created for a song—and the spatial positioning, equalization, echo, and other effects have been preset on the control board—the multitrack master is played back and all the individual channel levels are controlled during playback to create the musical blend or mix that the producer wants as the two mixed-down channel outputs are recorded on the two-track master tape. The only limits on the number of mix variations and permutations a producer can try in aiming for the optimum mix are those of time and studio cost. Once again, the producer is faced with the decision of when to declare the work finished and the mixdown complete and final.

It is important to note that the mixdown process cannot correct major flaws or alter special effects that were recorded on the original multitrack tape. If a guitar sound was fuzzed, limited, or predistorted during the original recording, the effect cannot be eliminated in remix. Such effects can be added during remix, however, should the producer wish to use them.

PRODUCTION WRAP-UP

When all session and mixdown work is done, the producer should play the final master tape to reconfirm the order and exact timing of selections, which may have changed as a result of editing processes. Exact timing is important to disc jockeys who give the record air play and, in selections more than 5½ minutes long, may affect the royalty rate. Timing information is also important to the mastering laboratory. The song list, with times, should clearly indicate the beginning and end of each side of a record.

All outtakes and significant editing clippings should be spliced together with a foot of paper leader tape between each piece of recorded tape. It is possible that at some later date it may prove desirable to revise the master tape or to release a different version of any tune recorded. This can be done if everything that was recorded during sessions is saved. The outtake reels should be marked and accompanied by complete notes as to what they contain. During recording and mixdown, most engineers keep a log for each tune on which console data is noted: pan pot positions, echo levels, channel levels, equalization, and the like. These logs should also be preserved.

The two-track master tape should have several feet of paper leader tape at the start (head) and the finish (tail), both of which should be marked accordingly. The leader should also be annotated with the record title, the name of the production organization, and the total duration of the recorded material (except level-set tones) from the first note of the first selection to the final fade on the last selection of each side. This includes the time duration—typically six to eight seconds—between successive tunes, which will have been programmed in by inserting blank leader tape between the selections. At least thirty seconds of each setup tone in the case of recordings made with noise reduction techniques, or thirty seconds of 1 kHz zero level, should be recorded and included between the head leader and the first selection. The master tape should be wound tail out on the reel(s) or hub(s) and repackaged in the appropriate tape container, which should be marked clearly and neatly with title, producer, production organization, studio, selection and time data, and the address and phone number of the engineer and producer to be contacted by the mastering lab or duplicating house in the event of questions.

The master tape should be wrapped carefully and boxed and sent to the mastering lab fully insured for the whole cost of production.

The people responsible for graphic arts require the exact

tune titles; the names of composers, authors, and publishers of tunes; the tune times; the correctly spelled names of all the artists, engineers, and production assistants; artist biographical notes; and producer's notes on any interesting events that occurred during production. This information will be used in part for label design and may also be used to prepare liner notes. In some modern music productions it may be useful to have song lyrics printed on the sleeve of an album; exact lyrics should also be furnished by the producer if this is contemplated.

If session times have overrun or underrun budget, the producer may need to have studio purchase orders and the contracts filed with the union for the amended sessions.

TEST RECORD APPROVAL

The last responsibility of a producer is often that of approving test records.

When a master tape is sent to a mastering laboratory, the laboratory can cut a reference lacquer at the same time the master lacquer is being cut. If two reference lacquers are ordered—and it is smart to do so unless the lab's work is intimately known—the producer can listen to one to confirm that the mastering lab has done nothing to impair the sound the producer labored to create in the studio. The other can be saved for future comparison with the test pressings.

Lacquers are soft and degrade rapidly with repeated playback, so the first playback should be done under ideal conditions in which the producer can listen with undivided attention and without distraction. If the lacquer plays satisfactorily, the master lacquer can be released to the plater. If not, the producer will have to discuss the matter with the mastering lab and continue to have lacquers cut until an acceptable version results.

The producer's final approval comes when the test pressings—a few records actually manufactured from production metalwork—are received from the pressing plant. If the reference lacquer was good, any deficiencies in the test pressings are probably attributable to the electroplating process. This is because the pressing plant is not likely to offer the very first pressings, which usually are unsatisfactory, to the producer for approval. When the producer okays the test pressing, the manufacturing run can be authorized.

If the end product is a cassette or eight-track tape, the producer should approve manufacturing samples before full-scale duplication is authorized.

5

Related Operations

Even though a master tape has been finished, there is some work to do before a salable product emerges from the production process.

MASTERING LABORATORY

The mastering laboratory—an independent operation, a part of a studio, or a part of a record manufacturing plant—transfers the master tape to the master lacquer disc.

There are two strongly contrasting points of view with respect to and within mastering laboratories. The first is that the lab should duplicate on the lacquer exactly what is on the master tape, reproducing the producer's studio effort as faithfully and precisely as art, science, and skill permit. This viewpoint comes mainly from overseas, especially from continental Europe. The second is that the mastering lab has as great a duty as anyone in the whole chain of production to contribute to the ultimate sound and marketability of the record. This American view is now spreading abroad.

The mastering lab is equipped with a tape player and a recording lathe. It is also equipped with equalizers, limiters, compressors, noise reduction devices, and reverb (echo) equipment in more or less direct proportion to the degree to which it subscribes to either of the foregoing viewpoints.

The basic task of the mastering lab is to manage the tape-to-disc transfer so that the groove can be tracked by home playback pickup arms without skipping. The next basic task is to equalize the disc recording so that there is the least loss of fidelity as the pickup stylus travels from the outside of the disc toward the smaller inside diameter, where high frequency response falls off and distortion increases. Most of the rest of what is possible in the mastering process is confined by, and interacts with, these two root requirements.

In mastering 45 rpm singles, a common objective for the mastering lab is the attainment of the producer's urgent plea to make his record hot—one that ideally will play louder on jukeboxes than other records. Since that is every producer's goal these days, from a practical viewpoint the job of the mastering lab is that of making the new recording no *less* loud than its competitors. With few exceptions, contemporary 45s are mastered for loudness at considerable expense with respect to distortion.

The other common objective is to produce a disc with maximum signal-to-noise ratio. Since the noise floor is fixed by residual groove noise with no signal present, the upper signal limit is the one that has to be stretched to provide the greatest dimension between minimum and maximum levels. The problem is essentially the same as that in making a hot 45, except that for albums listener tolerance for distortion is considerably lower. The degree of push is dependent on the musical material, ranging from fairly high for acid rock to almost nothing for pure classics.

Mastering lab engineers need to have, and do have, a high perception of how music reproduced from a disc will reach the listener's ears in typical situations. Youth market records are often played on portable or relatively inexpensive players with small, cheap loudspeakers. The lab engineer may boost the bass portion of the audio spectrum to ensure that the young audience will hear the bass and percussive rhythm that sells this sort of music. On pop or classical works, the same engineer would probably use far less extra equalization.

Half-speed mastering is a technique that is used by some labs to achieve extreme high-frequency response. Both the master tape playback recorder and the cutting lathe are operated at half the normal speed. Every recorded note is thus played back at half its original frequency, which makes it easier for the cutting head to swing the cutting stylus on the high-frequency material. The effect is audible, especially in material rich in harmonic content, but only barely.

The sacrifice involved in half-speed mastering is that it takes more than twice as long to cut a master lacquer because experimentation is required before appropriate level and equalization settings can be achieved. It may be necessary to cut and play several lacquers to reach the desired and required cutting parameters. The direct consequence is a significant increase in mastering cost. Half-speed mastering is a quality improvement technique that merits consideration for good material, especially that which may excite the audiophile/purist market.

It is important for a producer to convey to the mastering lab any particular goals that the mastering process is to achieve, especially if there are special instructions. For example, it is fairly common to make a monaural master of 45s from which promotional copies for distribution to mono-only AM radio stations will be pressed, in addition to the stereo master from which all other release copies will be derived. The lab will need to be told if such service is required. And while the master tape should have been finished in the studio to a degree of perfection at which no further adjustments are needed, the mastering lab *is* the last point at which any necessary improvement modifications can be made, so they should be made if necessary.

Concerned producers will be present during mastering even

if their responsibilities end contractually with delivery of the finished master tape. This is a matter of professional pride rather than of obligation but is subject to the policies of the lab; some laboratories bar outsiders from the cutting rooms. If a producer feels strongly about monitoring the cutting process, the point should be made clear when the lab is selected.

ELECTROPLATERS

The platers that make the metalwork for disc pressings may be either independent organizations or captive facilities within a record pressing plant. The basic processes of metalwork preparation were discussed in Chapter 2.

Older plating operations required up to twenty-four hours to complete each step of the process from lacquer master to stamper. Modern plating facilities use much faster plating methods, but at the cost of a higher residual groove noise (reduced signal-to-noise potential) and with a higher probability that minute plating bubbles, which produce audible ticks or stylus bounces, will result. Meticulous inspection of completed metalwork and delicate hand-tooled correction of minor defects are less common measures in high-speed plating operations than in those that continue to use older techniques.

The best plating work is generally but not invariably done by independent houses. When technical perfection is important to eventual product marketability, as is especially true with respect to direct-to-disc releases, the plater of choice will usually be one of the quality-oriented specialist houses rather than the captive facility of a volume-production-oriented pressing plant. There are two disadvantages in working with an independent plater: It takes longer to get from lacquer master to manufacturing metalwork, both because of the processes and because of the added logistical handling requirements. Also, responsibility for ultimate product quality is spread out. If there are quality problems, the plater may blame the pressing plant, and vice versa.

The added cost of high-quality metalwork is insignificant in all cases but that of records that are to be pressed in very small quantities (hundreds to a few thousands).

PRESSING PLANTS

Competition has driven virtually all pressing plants to automated machinery such as the injection molding equipment shown in Figure 5. These machines will produce one labeled and trimmed LP or two 45s in about 30 seconds. Finished product quality, as a result, depends on the following factors:

- The number of pressings made from each stamper
- The generation of the stamper
- Care in machine setup and operation
- Machinery maintenance
- Quality of vinyl (virgin or recycled) used to make pressings
- Postpressing inspection and quality assurance techniques

The record production company has virtually no control over what happens in the pressing plant, so its only protection lies in the provisions of its contract with the pressing plant with respect to return and remake of defective pressings, and its control over future business. If mastering and/or metalwork is done by organizations independent of the pressing plant, the purchase order to, or contract with, the pressing plant should provide for pressing plant acceptance and approval of these materials, and responsibility for the resultant product. It is very unlikely that a major label plant will alter its normal terms and do so.

The minimum manufacturing run for major label-associated pressing plants is typically 5,000 records. Independent plants will press as few as 100 records.

The product delivered by the pressing plant is finished ready-to-sell records. The sleeves and jackets may be furnished by the production company or may be obtained from the pressing plant by furnishing the necessary graphic artwork. If these materials are furnished by the production company, they must

FIGURE 5
Modern Record Pressing (Molding) Machine

(Courtesy Southern Machine & Tool Corporation)

reach the pressing plant in time to permit the smooth execution of the manufacturing operations. The pressing plant ordinarily prefers to have pressed records packaged with as little storage time and as few handling operations as possible and will not start pressing until all necessary components of the final product are on hand.

An important matter to consider when ordering records is the number of records per shipping carton. Forty-fives are generally packaged in boxes of 100, while LPs can be boxed 25, 50, or 100 per carton. The cost of albums packed in cartons of 25 may be higher than if packed in larger quantities, but this cost may be offset if the production company does not have to open cartons and repack for shipment to distributors or dealers.

The selected pressing plant should be required to send test pressings to the production company for approval before being permitted to begin volume manufacturing. If the pressing plant is also furnishing jackets, the production company may need to see and approve brownlines of artwork and color keys or press proofs of jacket art.

Although a production company can furnish the record labels to the pressing plant, this is usually done only on very large volume pressings or when the label itself is somehow very special. If a special label is envisioned, the production company should be sure to consult with the pressing plant on the plant's requirements for paper stock, dimensional control, printing ink, and the like before going ahead with manufacturing.

More frequently, the labels will be printed and furnished by the pressing plant. The producing company will have to supply either finished artwork or all the information needed to create finished artwork.

GRAPHICS DESIGN AND JACKET/CARTON MANUFACTURE

There are two basic kinds of jackets for record albums. The first is made of a single sheet of very heavy paper stock that is die-cut to provide glue tabs, then folded and glued to create the jacket. Jacket printing can be done either before or after the folding and gluing operation. These jackets are relatively inexpensive, and printed material is usually kept very simple—one or two colors, black-and-white reproduction of photographs, avoidance of artwork that requires critical color registration.

The more common album jacket is made by fabricating the basic jacket of cardboard, then gluing preprinted fronts and backs called *surrounds* or *wraps* onto the cardboard. This more complicated jacket has a much stiffer feeling and allows complete flexibility for use of four-color process printing, gold or other metallic embossing, and thermographic printing that creates raised letters. These jackets can be made for double-album sets. They can also be made more durable and more expensive-looking by coating the finished jacket with a varnish that is actually a clear acrylic.

Whatever is to appear on the final jacket, whether directly imprinted or printed on the wraparounds, is prepared as camera-ready art.

Jacket design usually begins with sketches of several possible approaches, which are prepared by the graphics manager, art director, or a commercial artist and are called *roughs*. The next step is usually to refine the rough into a semifinished art presentation called a *comprehensive,* or *comp,* in which everything is shown in appropriate color and position, but which excludes type and photographs. The next step is the camera-ready art itself, which consists of art board upon which all type from a typesetter, as repro proofs, is laid out in exact position. The positions for all other materials, such as drawings and photographs, are indicated in camera-invisible blue pencil in exact final size; this is called the *mechanical* or *keyline.* If the jacket is being printed in multiple colors, graphic elements may be positioned on clear overlays or acetates that are themselves positioned on the art board and held in place with masking tape. Any photography or other artwork that is to be stripped into the camera negatives or subsequent positives is mounted on art board. Crop marks outlining the exact area to be used and information on reduction (e.g., "reduce to 2½-inch height") are made, often on a tissue or vellum overlay. If special color ink is to be used in printing, colors are specified on the final art by reference to the Pantone or any other standard color matching system.

The time to proofread with meticulous care and to examine all artistic elements critically is while the artwork is in development and before it goes to the cameraman. It is downright embarrassing to discover a misspelled name or word, or to discover a disconcerting artistic element such as a tree apparently growing out of someone's head in a photograph, in a completed ready-to-sell album. Corrections made at this late point are also terribly expensive to make. In fact, the cost of correction rises at every step along the path, from art concept to finished, printed, assembled jacket.

The processes described above will occur whether the jacket is designed in house or is left to an outside source. Responsibilities for accuracy are scattered among producers, writers, typists, typesetters, artists, and camera operators and retouchers. In most cases the very last chance the producing company will have to fix graphic screw-ups before it becomes outrageously expensive to do so will occur when brownlines and/or color keys are presented for final preprinting approval. The brownlines are one-color reproductions of the composite of all negatives that will be used to make the printing plates. The color key consists of four pieces of film that, when assembled in register, will duplicate the full-color rendition of the printed product when viewed on a properly illuminated light board. It is supplied only when the jacket art is in full color. A more expensive alternative to the color key is a full-color press proof on paper.

The parties involved in generating artwork may be completely separate and independent businesses, or they may be combined in whole or in part under one roof. They include artists and layout artists; photographers; typographers; illustrators; and the color separator, which does the camera work and includes craftsmen known as strippers who strip in photographs and dot etchers who hand-correct any deficiencies in the negatives resulting from the photographic color separation processes.

The processes discussed are also applicable with respect to artwork for cassette or eight-track cartons.

The bare essentials for printed matter on jackets and labels, and elements that can be considered optional, are shown in Table 3.

TABLE 3

Description	MUST APPEAR ON Label	Jacket	MAY BE PUT ON Label	Jacket
Album title	X	X		
Name and address (at least city, state, and zip code; street or P.O. box may be required under some legal interpretations) of the producing activity, e.g., Whizbang Records, Inc., or J. Doe dba Whizbang Records	X	X		
Label name (e.g., WHIZBANG!)			X	X
Label or logotype trademark indicia if applicable (® or "Reg. U.S. Pat. Off." or ™ as appropriate—see below)	X	X	(X)*	(X)
Copyright notice if applicable, with name and date; e.g., © 1980 Whizbang Records, Inc.	X	X	(X)	(X)
"Manufactured and Printed in U.S.A."	X	X	(X)	(X)
"Warning: Unauthorized duplication is a violation of applicable federal, state, and international law."	X	X	(X)	(X)
Song titles (exact form)	X			X

Trademark indicia must *not* be used unless a trademark has been applied for or has been issued. It is appropriate to use ™ when the application has been filed with the U.S. Patent Office or a state government, or when the trademark has been certified by a state government. The only proper use of ® or "Reg. U.S. Pat. Off." is when the trademark has been registered with the U.S. Patent Office *and* the registration certificate has been received. The copyright indicator can be used as soon as the

Description	MUST APPEAR ON		MAY BE PUT ON	
	Label	Jacket	Label	Jacket
Song times			X	X
Names of composers, authors, publishers			X	X
Composer, author, publisher affiliation (e.g., ASCAP, BMI, etc.)			X	X
Names of musicians, producer, assistants, engineers, copyists, studios, marketing organizations, designers, graphic artists, photographers (cover art)			X	X
Names of arrangers, if AFM members (applies to single records only)	X		X	X
Record catalog number			X	X
"Stereo," "LP," or other indicator			X	X
Promotional ads or remarks				X
Liner notes				X
Dedications				X
Song lyrics				X

*Items in parentheses (X) must appear on the label and jacket to afford legal protection to the producing organization but are not absolutely required by law.

application for copyright has been filed with the Register of Copyrights. These statements apply only to U.S. trademarks and copyrights; foreign producers should determine applicable overseas law.

Notice that the product is manufactured and printed in U.S.A. is important if the records are exported. Records that are not so marked may be stopped at foreign customs or subjected to extra import duties. It doesn't cost anything to include the notice and there's no apparent reason why it should be omitted.

The warning about unauthorized duplication probably won't have any effect on private purchasers who make tape copies of the product, but it puts prospective commercial pirates on notice and will be beneficial if a pirating case has to be prosecuted criminally or if civil action is taken to enjoin further activity or recover damages.

When names of artists, composers, or others are used in print, be sure that they are spelled correctly. Song titles must not only be spelled correctly, they must be complete as contained in the mechanical rights license or copyright as well.

How much information to put on the album jacket, over and above that which needs to be included for legal reasons, is to some degree determined by the market. For example, jazz enthusiasts expect liner notes to give information about artists and material. Also, a direct-to-disc recording or any record embodying a new technical approach should describe the technology for audiophiles. And rock records may have to include printed lyrics because rock singing style does not emphasize understandability. X-rated lyrics should be printed only on album record sleeves, if at all.

If design or market considerations dictate the use of liner notes, consideration should be given to the choice of a writer. National or local reviewers, critics, or peer artists may be persuaded to write liner notes free of charge or for fees, depending on the circumstances. As a general rule, the more esoteric the content of the album, the more likely it appears to be that liner notes will help sell the product. Artist photographs

FIGURE 6
Jacket Artwork Layout

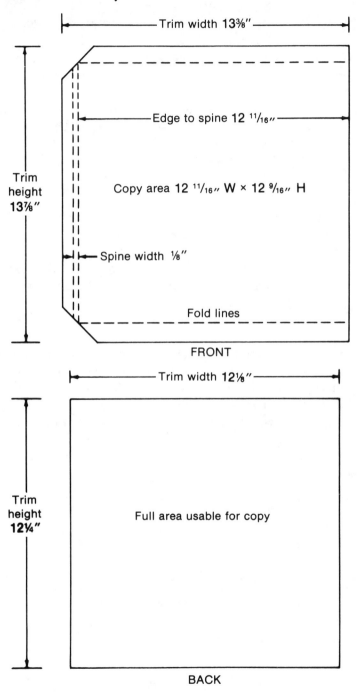

Trim width 13⅜"

Trim height 13⅞"

Edge to spine 12 ¹¹⁄₁₆"

Copy area 12 ¹¹⁄₁₆" W × 12 ⁹⁄₁₆" H

Spine width ⅛"

Fold lines

FRONT

Trim width 12⅛"

Trim height 12¼"

Full area usable for copy

BACK

help to sell only the work of well-known artists, and it is a mistake to use a performer photograph if the photo doesn't fit the title and material. For instance, an acid rock album should not include the photograph of any player who looks like a recruiting sergeant for "Today's Army."

A key point in graphic design for record albums is that the title or other vital selling information must be at the top of the album, where it can be seen quickly by a consumer who is flipping through record bins.

ARTWORK LAYOUT

Typical dimensions of the wraps for the front and back of a twelve-inch LP album are shown in Figure 6. The front and back copy areas are indicated. The front is pasted to the chipboard base first, and the flaps at the top, left, and bottom fold over to the back of the chipboard. The back is pasted on and conceals the foldovers. Artwork may be full bleed if desired, but no attempt should be made to match art front to back.

It is common practice to include an album number, its title, and the label name on the left-edge spine. The type should be no larger (taller) than eight-point News Gothic and should be centered in the available ⅛-inch spine width.

The layout artist should check with the printer and the converter/boxmaker to ensure that these suppliers use the normal assembly techniques to which the foregoing dimensional data apply.

6

Budget Preparation

The budget has been mentioned frequently in this book because it profoundly influences and interacts with every other aspect of record production. Discussions with new producers—and with several who have been in the business for quite some time—indicate that the monetary side of the business is one of its most mysterious and least understood aspects, even though money is almost always the yardstick by which success and failure are measured.

A budget is simply an economic game plan. If the game plan is followed in spite of all the pressures to deviate, at least the maximum amount of money that can be lost in an unsuccessful venture will be known up front. The best case benefit is that a runaway hit will have been produced at sensible and controlled cost, and profits will develop earlier and will be larger than they would have been if the record had been produced without fiscal restraint. Both sides of that coin are probably more important to an independent producer than they are to a major label with more or less unlimited resources at its disposal.

Accountants differentiate among different kinds of costs. The costs that will be discussed in this chapter are direct costs that are intimately associated with the production of a record, whether a disc or a tape. Established companies will have additional costs of an indirect nature, such as overhead, which are necessary to the operation of the business but do not have an immediate bearing on the record itself. Costs such as overhead and general and administrative expenses are commonly allocated pro rata by accountants to individual record production projects. Such costs, if they exist in the producing organization, must be added to the direct costs discussed here.

There are three reasons for preparing a budget.

First, when the estimated costs of producing a record are known, these costs can be compared with estimates of future income from sales to determine whether or not the production has a chance of economic success. If the number of records that must be sold to break even and begin to show a profit exceeds the number of records that can reasonably be expected to be sold, then the record is a candidate for economic failure. Foreknowledge of this prospect should lead to serious second thoughts on whether or not to proceed with the production at all.

Second, the budget indicates the amount of money that will be needed to complete the project and defines the amount of financing that will be required.

Third, the budget is a management tool. It defines the cost and performance targets for the producer and allows management to compare the actual costs of progress to any point with the amount that should have been spent to achieve that progress according to the budget plan, and to take action if necessary to keep cost and progress in step.

A basic rule of budget preparation is that the greater the degree to which elements of cost can be broken down into subcategories that can be individually estimated or priced out, the more accurate the total budget is likely to be when the whole job is finished. A road builder may toss out a figure of $2.5 million per mile as a ballpark estimate of the cost of constructing a section of highway. However, he will try to nail down the cost of the last bag of cement and man-hour of labor when preparing a bid for submission in competition against other road builders. In record production and road building, the reason for detailed estimating is the same: the process forces careful scrutiny and consideration in depth that helps to prevent the possibility of unpleasant cost surprises when the project is under way.

TALENT COSTS

For most record productions, the largest expenditures will be made for talent, including musicians, vocalists, music arrangers, and the producer. In most cases, only the producer will be nonunion. For everyone else, the cost buildup occurs within the framework of the applicable union agreements and recording session contracts.

Musicians

For musician members of the AFM, the key document is the Phonograph Record Labor Agreement between the company and the AFM. The PRLA establishes wage scales, work rules, and other cost bases. The current PRLA was negotiated between the AFM and signatory companies in October 1979 and covers a twenty-five-month period that began on November 1, 1979. The wage scales for recording for the first twelve months of the agreement are summarized in Appendix B. The indicated basic scales will increase by 7 percent for the thirteen months that begin on November 1, 1980.

The foundation of the wage scale concept on which the industry and the union have settled is that the amount of music that can be used from a given period of musician availability-to-perform is controlled. Thus, from a three-hour basic session during which a couple of hours of music might actually be recorded, the company is permitted to release no more than fifteen minutes of that music on the end product. If, through some extraordinary set of circumstances, enough high-quality music was played during a single three-hour session to fill a forty-five-minute-long album, the company would be obliged to pay the players for three full sessions. This root concept also applies to overtime: five minutes of recorded music can be extracted from the recordings made during each half hour of overtime, but only if the session is a *basic* session (more on this shortly). Overtime is the time by which scheduled sessions are extended and is not the same as premium time.

Regular basic sessions are those that take place between 8 A.M. and midnight on ordinary weekdays that are not holidays and between 8 A.M. and 1 P.M. on Saturdays that are not holidays. Sessions occurring at all other times except on holidays are sessions in premium time, for which the wage scale is 1½ times (150 percent) the rates applicable to regular basic sessions *and* the overtime associated with the sessions.

Regular basic session and associated overtime rates double for sessions that take place on New Year's Day, Washington's birthday, Memorial Day, Independence Day, Labor Day, Thanksgiving, and Christmas in the United States; and on New Year's Day, Good Friday, Easter Monday, Victoria Day, Dominion Day, Labour Day, Thanksgiving, and Christmas in Canada.

There are exceptions to the foregoing guidelines with respect to show albums and location (e.g., nightclub) albums and to royalty artists; these exceptions are described in the PRLA.

Three hours is the fixed duration of a regular basic session. The session must be scheduled in advance and cannot be canceled, postponed, or rescheduled less than seven days in advance. This does not mean that sessions must be scheduled a week in advance, only that the seven-day rule applies once they are scheduled. If there is a possibility that a scheduled session may involve more than a half hour of overtime, the company must advise the musicians of the possibility and the duration limit at the time of hiring.

These work rules are designed to force a company to take some calculated risks. Suppose that, at the end of a 3-hour basic session, only ten minutes of usable material has been recorded, but the company needs fifteen minutes to meet its objectives. If it has taken 3 hours to put ten minutes of music in the can, then it may take another 1½ hours to get the remaining five minutes. But that 1½ hours of extra time, if spent at overtime rates, will cost the same as another 3-hour basic session. The producer has a choice between continuing the session on an overtime basis or stopping and scheduling another basic session. If the material is obtained in less than 1½ hours, overtime will be less expensive than another basic session. But if it takes more than 1½ hours to get the extra five minutes, the company would have been better off scheduling another basic session, during which it would have had a full 3 hours of musician availability to fulfill its needs.

Two other work rule elements of the PRLA reflect the changes that have occurred in recording technology with the advent of tape recording and multitrack recording.

In regular time, premium time, or on a holiday, no more than four sides or album segments may be sweetened during a basic session. The sides or segments to be sweetened must have been recorded at a previous session.

If a musician does tracking—that is, if the musician goes back to play harmony or other music to tracks that he or she had previously recorded so that the final recording includes both the original and the tracking performances—the musician is paid for each additional track laid to create the sound of additional instrumentation as though separate musicians had been used for those parts.

Tracking is not the same as doubling. If a musician plays two or more instruments during a session—switching, for example, from sax to clarinet—the first extra instrument earns a premium of 20 percent of applicable scale. Other extra instruments earn a premium of 15 percent of applicable scale for the player. The PRLA defines carefully which instruments do and do not count as doubles.

The other cost-impacting aspects of the PRLA are the provisions with respect to cartage; the requirement that the company contribute 10 percent of the scale wages of musicians, including doubling, to the AFM-EPW Fund and $3.75 per musician per session to Health and Welfare; and those provisions that make the company an employer, with the obligations that role dictates vis-à-vis payroll taxes, workmen's compensation, unemployment insurance, and the like.

If a company is paying overscale to musicians, it may not make any difference whether the session occurs during premium time periods or on holidays. But if musicians are engaged for sessions at scale, it is clearly advantageous for the company to schedule all sessions, including overtime, so that they occur during regular session time limits, and to cluster all tunes that will require doubling into as few sessions as possible, since doubling is figured on a per-session basis.

The factors that influence the amount of session time required include the nature and complexity of the music to be performed, how tightly it's arranged, the proficiency of the players, the number of players (chances for player error and spoiled takes increase as the group size increases), the extent to which the material has been rehearsed, and human factors such as artist temperament and the ability of the group leader and the producer to manage the sessions so that everything stays on track.

The PRLA allows fifteen minutes of music to be extracted from a three-hour basic session, which is a ratio of twelve minutes of composite playing, playback, coffee break, talkover, and retake time to each minute of releasable music. The actual production ratio can vary widely for differences in the factors mentioned above. A well-rehearsed solo pianist may turn out a forty-minute album in no more time than it takes to sit down, let the engineer get his or her levels, and play the music. A complex production involving an instrumental group, on the other hand, could average far less than the allowable output.

The amount of session time budgeted should be based on careful evaluation of the specific situation and should be figured on the generous side to accommodate the unexpected and unforeseeable. For all but solo performers and very well-rehearsed small groups such as duos and trios, the ratio of planned session time to usable music should be at least fifteen to one. A production ratio as high as sixty to one (i.e., an hour of session time for one minute of usable output) may be justifiable. Higher ratios suggest the need for better planning or rehearsal.

The session time budget naturally depends somewhat on the producer's experience and familiarity with the artists, engineers, and their skills. In addition, session time planning must take into account the situation in which basic, vocal, and sweetening may be done at separate sessions and possibly at different studios, with different personnel in different locations. The whole idea is to plan the production as carefully and fully as is practical so that the resulting budget will be sufficient to cover the costs. It is infinitely better to underspend the available money than to run out of money before the production is finished.

The caliber of the musicians has a real impact on planning. Don Ewell, the legendary pianist with the Jack Teagarden and Dukes of Dixieland bands, recounts turning out master tapes for three complete albums in just under nine hours with his quartet. Other topflight pros report similar experiences, and the fact that you are working with seasoned, confident players (who are seldom prima donnas) can certainly be considered in the planning and budgeting process, if such is the case.

The time budget must be converted into a dollar estimate, and the Musician Cost Estimate Worksheet in Figure 7 can be used for this purpose.

A hypothetical album will be used to illustrate the process of cost workup. Assume that the album will be cut by an established, well-rehearsed group of six players, including the leader. Assume also that the sessions can all be scheduled during nonpremium time, that one of the instruments is a stand-up bass (a cartage instrument), and that there is no doubling, tracking, or travel involved. Finally, assume that the album is to have forty minutes of music and that all musicians work for scale.

The album described is a straightforward one, with no

FIGURE 7

MUSICIAN COST ESTIMATE WORKSHEET

	No. of Men	No. of Basic Sessions	Rate/Basic Session	Total Basic Session Cost	No. of ¼-Hrs. Overtime	Overtime Rate	Total OT Cost	TOTAL COST
Leader	1	3	274.43	823.29	4	45.75	183.00	1,006.29
Contractor								
Sidemen	5	3	137.21	2,058.21	20	22.87	457.40	2,515.55
Tracking Sidemen								
First Doubles								
Additional Doubles								

Total Base Wages 3,521.84

Employer's (only) portion of Federal FICA, FUT and similar state taxes at 9 % rate estimated   316.97

Company contribution to AFM-EPW Fund at 10 % of Total Base Wages   352.18

Health and Welfare at $ 3.75 per person (incl. Contractor) per Basic Session   67.50

Travel Expenses payable/reimbursible to musicians, including per diem costs

Instrument Cartage (list instruments) BASS VIOL   18.00

TOTAL ESTIMATED COST $ 4,276.49

Notes:
1) Contractor required on all sessions with 12 or more sidemen. Contractor may be a sideman and is paid at same scale as leader.
2) Calculate tracking and doubling charges only for sessions in which they occur (not necessarily all sessions).
3) Use additional sheets to calculate wages for premium night and holiday sessions, if applicable.
4) Calculate AFM-EPW contribution on basis of minimum scale (not actual wages) for overscale musicians.

elaborations such as tracking, and the group is said to be well rehearsed in the material to be performed. It is reasonable in these circumstances to use a conservative production ratio of fifteen to one for session time, so the budget time is 40 minutes of releasable music times 15, which equals 600 minutes, or ten hours, of session time. The efficient way to schedule this time would be through three basic sessions, with one hour of overtime on the final session.

Scale for the leader is $274.43 for each basic session and $45.75 for each fifteen minutes of overtime.

Because this recording involves fewer than twelve sidemen, a contractor is not required. If a contractor were to be used, the scale would be the same as for the leader. If a contractor is also a sideman, the only extra compensation for such a person would be made for extra services such as doubling.

The other five people in the group are sidemen, for whom scale is $137.21 each per basic session and $22.87 for each fifteen minutes of overtime. There will be twenty quarter hours of planned overtime for the sidemen.

As the employer of the musicians, the company will have to pay the usual business contributions for Social Security (FICA) and unemployment (FUT). In many states the employer is required to withhold and contribute to other social or tax funds. The amount entered for these taxes should be limited to the amount that the employer pays as its share, not amounts that the musician-employees pay through withholding. An accountant should be consulted to determine the applicable rates in your state and under current federal law. The reason for including only the company's share is that this reflects the company's actual out-of-pocket cost. Money that is withheld from net payments to musicians is merely collected by the company from the musicians and passed on to the applicable tax authorities.

For illustrative purposes it has been assumed that the employer's tax contributions in this case will be about 9 percent of the total base wages.

Under the PRLA, the employer will contribute 10 percent (current rate) of base wages to the AFM-EPW Fund.

For each basic session the employer will pay $3.75 per musician, including the leader, for Health and Welfare. In some union jurisdictions, this payment is made to the local. In others it is paid directly to the musicians. The contribution in the example is based on three (sessions) times six (players) times $3.75 = $67.50.

If any of the musicians were brought in from out of town, their travel and per-diem expenses would be included in the estimate.

The string bass is a cartage instrument, and the bass player will bring it to the studio three times. The extra compensation to that player for cartage is $6 per session.

The total projected musician cost for this particular album is $4,276.49.

While no tracking is contemplated for this album, it is useful to remember that when a musician does track, it is as if that person were an additional player (leader or sideman). It is generally best to schedule tracking work as separate sessions for the individuals involved rather than to do any tracking while the rest of the musicians are sitting and waiting while being paid.

If any musicians double, it is best to do all the tunes that require doubling in a single session, since doubling is paid for on a per-session basis. That is, once a musician has doubled on a session, however briefly, he is entitled to the premium pay for having doubled for the entire session, including any overtime associated with that session.

The material presented thus far relates to the sessions that are most likely to be undertaken by an independent producing company. A different scale applies to symphonic recording. There is also a *special session* scale that provides for 1½ hours, from which 7½ minutes of music may be used. The session is restricted to the cutting of no more than two sides and cannot be used to sweeten. The maximum permissible overtime is a half hour. The scale rates for special sessions are 32 percent higher on a per-hour basis than they are for regular basic sessions. The special session is primarily useful for cutting a 45 rpm single with a well-rehearsed group.

Another scale arrangement is available for use when dealing with individual musicians or with musicians who are part of a "recognized self-contained group." The artist or group must be under contract to the record company, and the contract must provide that the artist or group is to be paid royalties of at least 3 percent of the suggested list price of the record for (effectively net) records sold. Under this provision, each "royalty artist" is paid basic session scale for *each song*. But, there is no limit on the number of sessions that may be held, there is no overtime, and there are neither restrictions on nor extra payments for doubling, sweetening, or playing multiple parts. This arrangement is not optional. If the artists are royalty artists by definition, then this is the applicable scale. The arrangement does not apply to extra players who may join a group for recording purposes only and who are not covered by either individual or group contracts that provide for the minimum royalty rate mentioned above.

Royalties are not included on the worksheet because these costs are associated only with records sold after production is complete and records have been manufactured.

Vocalists

Instrumentalists who sing are paid only as musicians, not as vocalists. Singing by instrumentalists is not considered a double.

Singers who are members of the American Federation of Television and Radio Artists (AFTRA) are covered by the minimum wage scale and performance terms contained in AFTRA's Code of Fair Practice for Phonograph Recordings.

As with instrumentalists, vocalists may require payment at rates greater than scale.

The AFTRA code provides for scale on an hourly or per-side

basis, whichever results in the higher compensation, subject to a per-call minimum. A side is basically one song or medley of 3½ minutes or less, with a scale premium of 50 percent payable for each minute or fraction of a minute beyond the first 3½ minutes.

The basic scales under the code through March, 1981, are shown in Table 4.

TABLE 4

Number of Singers in Group	Rate per Person per Side or Hour	Minimum Call (2 sides or 2 hours)
Soloists and Duos	$100.00	(not stated, effectively $100)
3 to 8	38.00	$76.00
9 to 16	30.50	61.00
17 to 24	26.75	53.50
25 to 35*	22.75	45.50
36 or more*	19.25	38.50

*Nonclassical

The rates above are provisional. Although AFTRA and the recording industry held negotiations in the spring of 1980, the above rates had not been ratified by AFTRA's membership by October, 1980, and the union planned to re-open negotiations. Similarly unsettled are the increases (cumulative) of 5 percent and 7 percent in the above rates which were to have become effective in April of 1981 and 1982, respectively.

The disagreement between AFTRA and industry did not result in a strike (as of October, 1980) because industry agreed to pay not less than the negotiated rates until such time as a final contract could be worked out. It appears unlikely that industry will accept any retroactive increase in rates, but there is a real possibility that the escalation rates indicated above may change. A revised Code may also contain new provisions to interrelate music originally produced for television to the phonograph Code.

When a final settlement is reached, all the new scales, terms, and conditions will be printed in a new Code booklet, which will be available from AFTRA, 1350 Avenue of the Americas, New York, NY 10019.

The premium pay for work on Saturdays, Sundays, and holidays, and between 1 A.M. and 6 A.M. on weekdays is $5 per hour or fraction thereof.

There are also premiums and minimums for soloists and duos from within a group who "step out" (i.e., are featured) for some portion of a song, for singing a capella or in support of an orchestra on classical works, and for original-cast show albums. The work rules are complicated, and the Code (and probably an AFTRA representative) should be consulted for details on these unusual cases if they are expected to occur in a planned album.

A contractor is required whenever a vocal group consists of three or more people. The contractor must be an AFTRA member and one of the singers and is paid in addition to basic scale, per side or per hour, on the basis of the size of the group. (See Table 5.) There is an exception to the rule that the contractor must be a performer in a singing group which applies when the "sex of the group precludes the utilization of the contractor's singing services."

TABLE 5

Group Size	Contractor's Premium
3 to 8	$19.00
9 to 16	23.75
17 to 24	28.25
25 to 35	34.75
36 or more	41.25

The contractor scales above are also provisional and are subject to the same provisional escalation rates applicable to basic scales for singing.

In addition to wages, the company must pay 8½ percent of actual gross compensation to AFTRA's Pension and Welfare Fund. This arrangement differs from that of the AFM in that the payment is based on virtually every payment the company may ever make to the artist, including future royalties earned, salaries, fees, advances, guarantees, and even profit-sharing. The limitation is that the contribution is required for only the first $100,000 per year paid to an artist or an organized group. For budgeting purposes, a company would use scale wages as the basis for estimating production cost unless it plans to pay up-front compensation in a form other than, or in addition to, wages.

The Code, like the PRLA, also makes provisions for royalty artists. The arrangement is limited to groups made up of two or more people. If the contract with the group includes a royalty agreement (no minimum royalty rate is established), then the maximum amount payable per side is three times the per-side rate, no matter how many times the side must be recorded or how long it takes to record it.

Singers, like instrumental musicians, are made employees of the company under the AFTRA rules, and the company is obliged to make payroll deductions and contributions for taxes and the like as discussed under the heading "Musicians" earlier in this chapter.

Singers who do tracking, such as singing harmony parts to previous tracks they had recorded, are paid for tracking as if they were additional performers.

How long it will take singers to do their parts on a record depends on the same kinds of factors that pace the decisions of musician time estimates: familiarity with material, degree of rehearsal, and the like. In addition, it is necessary to think in terms of the vocalist(s) roles—star, chorus, background singers—and how they will be used (e.g., live with the band or in separate sweetening or vocal-add sessions). And it is necessary to conform the sides/time equation for singers with the usable music/time relationship applicable to instrumental musicians, since the two unions do not have compatible work rules.

One practical approach to vocalist costing is to do a calculation for each selection on a record that contains a vocal. For illustration, consider a four-minute tune on which three background singers will sing "doo-waah"s.

All three singers would be paid $38.00 for the side plus another $19.00 for the thirty seconds of music beyond the initial 3½ minutes. The individual serving as contractor would be entitled to another $19.00 for that service, so the total cost would be three times $38.00 plus three times $19.00 plus $19.00 equals $190.00. Again, using 9 percent as the estimated rate for employer contributions to payroll taxes and 8½ percent as the contribution to the AFTRA Pension and Welfare Fund (17½ percent total), the total projected vocal cost for that selection would be $223.25.

If only that one song were being augmented with a vocal, the cost would be higher because the minimum per-call rate would prevail over the per-side or per-hour rate.

When each selection that is to include vocals has been costed out, the total of all such costs should be included in the final production budget worksheet.

While the costs listed above are part of the production budget, it should be noted that the AFTRA code also provides for additional compensation to vocalists based on later record sales. This compensation becomes due only at the point at which sales of records reach the hundreds of thousands. Trigger points are 320,000 for original cast albums, 157,500 for other albums, and 500,000 for singles. These result in maximum additional payments to nonroyalty artists of 1.3, 2.0, or 1.67 times the original basic vocalist scale for the sessions from which the records emanated. Since these costs are contingent upon sales, they are not included in the production budget.

Music Preparation

The Phonograph Record Labor Agreement provides a very complex scale for music preparation, including arrangements, orchestrating, and copying. As a practical matter, these scales are of little use to the producing company for planning purposes since they require more advance knowledge of what the ultimate arrangements will consist of than the company has at the time that discussions relating to music preparation occur.

For budgeting, the best bet is to select an arranger and define exactly what is needed in terms of tunes, planned timing, desired sound, contemplated make-up of the musical group (which the arranger may recommend be altered, expanded, or reduced, based on other information), and the extent to which arrangements are needed (full charts, intros and riffs only, etc.). From this information, the arranger should provide a price package for delivery of finished arrangements, fully copied, and ready to use. The minimum cost for arranging a ten-stave score is roughly $3 per measure (bar) plus about 45¢ per measure for each instrument or other single-stave part copied. Again, these are minimums; actual charges can easily run much higher.

Music preparation services are also subject to the AFM-EPW Fund and Health and Welfare Fund contributions. The arranger, who should also furnish the subquotations from copyists who will prepare parts from his or her work, should be asked to indicate clearly all amounts in excess of charges for actual services that the producing company will be required to pay. If the company will be required to pay payroll taxes, the employer's share should be calculated exactly as in the case of musicians.

For the hypothetical album, it is assumed that the group is recording material from its "book," already arranged.

STUDIO COSTS

Studio charges are based on time, facilities used, and materials consumed. The studio cost for a location session, such as recording a live concert, may also include separate charges for mileage of the mobile recording van, travel, and per-diem charges for engineers.

Time Charges

There is usually a minimum time for which a studio can be reserved; two hours is typical. The time is usually charged in quarter- or half-hour increments beyond the minimum scheduled time. Overtime commonly applies to night, weekend, and holiday sessions, but this is negotiable. Musicians are generally allowed access to the "room" (the performing area, as differentiated from the control room or booth) thirty minutes before the scheduled session time so that they can set up instruments and warm up. A busy studio, however, may require that all access time be paid for; this should be checked when estimating studio time.

For a mobile van, there are generally two rates: one that applies during travel, another that applies when this recording equipment is operating.

There should be no reason to include possible cancellation charges in the cost estimate, but it should be kept in mind that such charges can be incurred if a session is canceled less than twenty-four, forty-eight, or seventy-two hours in advance, depending on the studio.

Studio time charges are based on the kind of recording equipment to be used. They are lowest for monaural recording and highest for the multitrack recorder with the most tracks. Services of the studio engineer(s) are covered in the time rates.

Typical time rates are shown in Table 6.

TABLE 6

Equipment	Live Recording	Mixdown/Edit/Transfer
Monaural, 2-track, or 4-track	$ 25–$65	$25–$55
8-track	50–100	35–85
16-track	75–125	60–100
24-track	85–150	80–125
32-track and up	100–175	90–140

Many studios offer discounts from their printed price list rates for block-time bookings in which the record company guarantees to pay for a minimum number of hours (commonly 10 hours) and/or to use those hours of reserved time in accordance with some predetermined schedule. The discounts range from about 10 percent for a ten-hour consecutive block to about 25 percent for a block of 100 hours that must be used within a period of a month.

The considerable spread of rates is not strictly attributable to the amount or quality of the equipment the studio has. The major influence on differences in the cost of similarly equipped studios is the degree of local competition, but a studio's current reputation for contributing to hit records can also have an effect on its rates. There is no doubt that hot producers and hot studios have a magnetic attraction for each other that filters into the rate cards of those studios.

Studio rates and terms are often negotiable.

Paying a premium price for studio work does not guarantee hit records, but it generally does assure that the studio will do a first class technical job and that its equipment will be very well maintained. While a studio will not charge for time needed to repair any equipment that breaks down during a session, neither will it reimburse the company for the continuing costs of musicians who are waiting for those repairs to be completed.

Studio cost is the second-largest expense (after talent) in most productions, and it is worthwhile to shop. Given comparable facilities and capabilities, the choice should lie with the studio that has an engineer who knows and has successfully recorded *your* kind of music.

Facility Charges

Use of the studio piano is free, and some studios also offer free use of a celeste or harpsichord if available. Some studios also provide a basic drum kit, for which they may have developed refined miking techniques, at no extra cost.

Other equipment items can either be included in the basic

studio charges or treated as separate billing items. These items can include synthesizers, electric pianos, harps, and electronic equipment such as echo chambers or reverberation devices, multitrack Dolby™ or other noise reduction systems, phasers, and flangers.

Studios with several performance rooms charge different rates for different rooms, usually expressed as a surcharge over the cost of the smallest room.

All facility costs should be included in the budget to the extent of planned use. For example, if a studio-rented synthesizer is going to be used for only one session, do not include the rental cost for all sessions.

Tape

If recording tape is furnished by the studio, the cost will be approximately $20 for ¼-inch, $35 for ½-inch, $50 for 1-inch, and $100 for 2-inch reels of 2,400 feet. Each reel will accommodate thirty minutes of recording at 15 inches per second recording speed or fifteen minutes at 30 inches per second speed.

The amount of tape that will be used depends on the way the producer works. Some producers save every take and even the false starts on "busted" takes on the theory that having a complete inventory of performed material may save the day during later editing sessions. In an effort to cut tape cost to the bone, other producers have the recorder backed up and record over everything that does not seem usable at the moment. The smartest approach is to save everything that is good, even if incomplete, and to record over everything that is obviously bad or unusable.

The recorder is not running all the time that players are in the studio. Time for talk-overs, quick rehearsals of difficult phrases, coffee breaks, and the time spent in listening to playbacks is not recording time in which tape is consumed. For budgeting purposes, figure five minutes of tape for each minute of planned release material for live recording, plus tape for the mixed-down master on multitrack sessions.

If a session is being recorded direct-to-disc, a two-track tape should be made simultaneously. One reason for doing this is that the tape is a backup from which a conventional record may be assembled if the direct-to-disc session doesn't work out. The second reason is that if the market for a record released direct-to-disc outlasts the metalwork from which those discs are pressed, the market may still survive for a conventional release of the same material. Be sure to allow for these tape costs in direct-to-disc sessions.

If work-print tapes are made, also include these costs.

Some studios permit the producer to supply tape instead of buying it from the studio. The wholesale cost of tape will be 25 to 30 percent less than the studio rate, but it is important that the tape be the same type and brand for which the studio is set up. If a different formulation is supplied, the studio's extra setup and recalibration charges may wipe out any savings.

Estimating Studio Time

The time estimate for live recording should be the same as that calculated for musician presence.

In addition, time must be budgeted for postproduction work such as mixdown, editing, sequencing, and tape transfers. The producer must listen to all the recorded takes to select the best complete takes or parts of takes that will be edited together to make a final take. If the recording was done multitrack, the producer will play material back several times, even many times, to arrive at the best mixdown levels, final equalization, and effects.

The best way to handle the postproduction time estimate is to obtain a commitment from the producer as to the amount of time that will be required. If the producer cannot or will not provide such a commitment, then the only alternative is to fix the allowable time arbitrarily. For the simple case of editing and sequencing an album that has originally been recorded direct-to-two track, allowing eight to twelve hours is reasonable. For a complex multitrack mixdown, edit, and transfer, a budget of one-half hour of postproduction studio time for each minute of releasable material is fairly conservative. Two hours of studio time per minute of material is fairly generous.*

Continuing with the example of the hypothetical album discussed earlier, calculations for studio time and cost are shown in Figure 8, a sample studio cost worksheet. It is assumed that the recording will be done on an eight-track machine and that Dolby™ will be used. It is also assumed that there will be ten hours of studio time for live recording and twenty hours for remix and edit (using the formula of a half hour of mixdown to each minute of releasable material, which is reasonable for eight-track).

The worksheet illustrated here may have to be modified to reflect the manner in which different studios charge, but the idea is to anticipate and log all the costs. The worksheet indicates that there might be a different studio time rate for playback only. This is true for some but not all studios.

MASTERING CHARGES

Basic costs for mastering range from about $50 to $100 per side for albums and a little less for 45s. Reference lacquers made at the same time as the master on another lathe or in succession with the same mastering control setup in labs with just one lathe cost $15 to $30 per side.

While only two masters are needed for a record, the first set may not necessarily meet the producer's requirements. For budgeting purposes it is a good idea to allow for two or more sets for complex material. Since all the metalwork for all the pressings will be generated from the master lacquers, this is no place to skimp.

---

*These times bear no relationship to the times some major labels have tolerated from some producers. One noted producing team claims to have spent 1,800 hours mixing and editing one album. It is the author's opinion that such producers are riding a gravy train that is going to come to an abrupt halt as the economic pressures on the record business continue to mount.

FIGURE 8

STUDIO COST WORKSHEET

COST SOURCE	QUANTITY	UNIT	UNIT COST	TOTAL	TAX?
Setup charges	3	SESSIONS	15	45	✓
Time charges					
Recording (straight time)	10	HOURS	75	750	✓
Recording (overtime)					
Playback only					
Mixdown, edit	20	HOURS	50	1000	✓
Mobile/location units					
Technical surcharges (echo, noise reduction, etc. List.)					
DOLBY	30	HOURS	15	450	✓
Instrument rentals (Arp, Moog, etc. List.)					
ELEC. PIANO	10	HOURS	10	100	✓
Tape (Indicate width. 2,400-foot reels unless otherwise indicated.)					
Basic sessions __1__ inch	7	REELS	50	350	✓
Sweetening _____ inch					
Remix, dubbing _____ inch					
Final master __¼__ inch	2	REELS	20	40	✓
Travel expenses					
Mobile unit mileage					
Personnel travel					
Personnel per diem					
Other studio charges (List.)					

Subtotal 2,735

Sales tax on checked items at __4__ percent   109

TOTAL 2,844

If the end product is to be cassette or eight-track, the cost of making the duplicating master tapes will normally be included in the product charge.

ARTWORK COSTS

Artwork is required for record, cassette, and eight-track labels, as well as for album jackets, tape cartons, and printed sleeves for 45s.

As noted earlier, it is possible simply to furnish typed instructions and copy for imprints and to have any of the printed material requirements fulfilled by a firm that specializes in record package design and manufacture. Such firms will provide design, layout, printing, and fabrication service on a turnkey basis. If this approach is taken, all needed budget information will be provided by the supplier in the form of a quotation.

At the other end of the spectrum, the company may make all the arrangements for packaging. In this case, the artwork may be done by an in-house artist, an ad agency, or a commercial artist. The objective is to come up with camera-ready art that can be turned over to the printer.

The cost of printed material depends primarily on the ultimate quantity ordered and the number of colors printed. For illustration, 1,000 album jackets printed on both sides in one color (e.g., black ink, although any single color may be chosen) will cost roughly 30¢ each. A thousand jackets in full color will cost roughly 50¢ each. For 10,000, the respective prices will be about 15¢ and 25¢. Price is also sensitive in smaller quantities to the complexity of the artwork, with more cost for art that includes both line (e.g., type and ink drawings) and halftone (e.g., photographs) materials. These prices do not include the cost of the camera-ready art.

In budgeting artwork, then, some thought must be given to later eventual cost as well as to the present cost of the camera-ready art, which is part of the production expense. It should be noted that very handsome artwork can be done in one color; however, color will usually help draw attention to one album in a rack of many at the retail store.

FIGURE 9

ARTWORK PREPARATION WORKSHEET

COST SOURCE	COST
Creative Services	
Basic design and rough sketches	$ _____
Comprehensive of selected design	_____
Original artwork (paintings, drawings)	_____
Photography (jacket, carton subject matter)	_____
Writer's charges (liner notes, other copy)	_____
Related Services	
Typography and typesetting	_____
Photoreduction or blowup (photostats)	_____
Layout and pasteup	_____
Brownlines (keylines)	_____
Other Services and Materials (list)	
_____	_____
_____	_____

TOTAL ESTIMATED COST

Note: Prepare separate worksheets for album jackets, printed sleeves, tape cartons, and record and tape labels.

The costs to be included in the production budget, as differentiated from manufacturing, are those through camera-ready art plus the cost of optional color separations. To maintain the highest quality control over the artwork that goes to the printer, the art director may decide to have color separations made by an independent specialist rather than by the printer. In this case, the cost of the separations goes into the production budget instead of being allocated as a manufacturing cost. Liner note costs can be included in the artwork budget.

An artwork cost worksheet is provided below (see Figure 9). Artists and agencies use different ways of quoting their services; for example, by charging for time and materials or on a flat-fee basis, so the buildup of cost is not indicated. But the several elements that must be included in the final composite of individual or lump quotations or estimates are shown.

PRODUCTION BUDGETS

The estimates and quotations discussed so far in this chapter can now be used to assemble two budgets. The first is the financial budget, which defines how much money will be needed to pay all the direct out-of-pocket expenses of production. The second is the producer's budget, which is the cost target for the efforts that are under the producer's control and supervision.

Costs of talent, studio, and music preparation are taken from the worksheets and quotations and are inserted in both the financial and producer's columns of the production budget worksheet (see Figure 10). The producer does not control the artwork, so this cost is entered only in the financial budget column.

These costs both involve creative processes for which costs cannot usually be exactly predicted. Because the numbers reflect educated guesses, some allowance needs to be made for the very real possibility of error. This is done by inserting a contingency allowance. The amount of the allowance should be in the range of 5 to 15 percent, with the final figure based on the degree of confidence that management and the producer have in the cost estimates and quotes. If confidence is so low that a figure higher than 15 percent is asked for, it is a sign that the planning was not thorough enough and should trigger a reassessment of the underlying quotes and estimates.

In each case, the contingency is attributed only to the costs of creative efforts in each column. The remaining costs should be quite firm so that no contingency allowance is needed for them.

FIGURE 10 — PRODUCTION BUDGETS

COST SOURCE		FINANCIAL		PRODUCER'S
Musicians (from worksheet)		$ 4,276		$ 4,276
Vocalists (from work-up)		—		—
Music prep (from work-up)		—		—
Studio (from worksheet)		2,844		2,844
Artwork (from worksheet)		1,148		
Subtotal		8,268		7,120
Contingency allowance	(10 %)	827	(10 %)	712
Lacquer masters (2 SETS)		300		—
Royalty advances to artists		—		
to producer		2,000		
Producer's fee		—		
Indirect costs		—		
		11,395		7,832

If the producer is to have the responsibility of selecting the mastering lab and approving lacquer masters, the cost of masters should be included in both columns. If the producer's effort is to be considered complete with delivery of master tapes, then the lacquer costs only go in the financial column.

Royalty advances to artists or to the producer are customarily recoverable from future sales; that is, when the records are sold, royalties due are used to offset advances until they are repaid. However, since advance money will be a direct expense during the production phase, it is an amount that must be included in the financial budget column. Royalties are not a part of the producer's budget.

If the producer is getting an up-front fee and/or expenses in addition to, or in lieu of, future royalties, the front money will also have to be available. The amount of the producer's fee belongs only in the financial column.

Earlier in this chapter, it was noted that organized and going companies will probably have a variety of indirect overhead and/or general and administrative costs. If these are allocated on a project basis, they should be included in the financial cost column. In small companies and partnerships, costs like these tend to be informally absorbed temporarily by the individuals who make up and participate in the venture and are handled later as expense account items.

MANUFACTURING COSTS

The cost elements listed above take us to the point at which tapes or records can be manufactured, but they do not include any manufactured product.

The next step(s) depend on how the company wants to work. The simplest approach is to pack up the master tape and the final artwork (either camera-ready or color separations) and send it to a pressing plant or tape duplicator that will take responsibility for all the remaining steps of manufacturing and packaging. Or the company can continue to control each step. Or it can control some of the steps and farm out the responsibility for others.

The factors that guide the decisions on these points are speed at which the project gets into production, the quantity of pressings or tapes to be ordered, the overall quality of the final product, and the logistics.

Considering the last point first, it is easy to find all the services involved in manufacturing in New York, Chicago, Los Angeles, and some other cities. When this is so, the company can farm out plating, pressing, printing, fabrication, and duplication to specialists in each field and can supervise, monitor, or inspect conveniently at each point of processing. Local shipping and delivery between plants is usually convenient, fast, and safe. If a company is physically located in one of the major metropolitan areas, or if it can send people to work with a number of vendors, shopping for each required service can provide significant cost advantages if the quantities are large. The savings involved in working with separate vendors can disappear quickly, however, and the risks of loss, damage, or inability to assign specific responsibility can increase, as can the time required to reach finished product, if the individual vendors are scattered across the country.

For relatively small quantities—hundreds to several thousands—very little, if anything, can be saved by dividing the manufacturing among many vendors. The only valid reason for doing so would be for quality control. This is a very good reason with respect to the plating and pressing of direct-to-disc records, but it is difficult to justify when small quantities are involved.

Every aspect of manufacturing, except for plating and metalwork preparation, is very sensitive to quantity. In small quantities, setup charges—whether quoted directly or buried in the cost quoted for product—escalate unit costs. In very large quantities, competition among vendors keeps costs down. A quantity of 100 twelve-inch records will cost about $2.50 each just for the discs—with no jackets, sleeves, or shrink wrap. For a quantity of 10,000, the price drops to around 47¢ each.* Prices do not decrease much further with increasing quantity because few added economies are available to the supplier beyond this point.

If records are produced in large quantities, creation of the metalwork is almost always left up to the pressing plant, and the quoted record price usually includes the necessary masters, mothers, and stampers. For high-quality or short runs, metal-

---

*Records and tapes are made of petroleum-based plastics. As oil prices rise, so will product costs.

work ordered from a specialty vendor will cost $18 to $25 per piece. For a run of 10,000 pressings, for example, with an imposed limit of no more than 2,000 pressings to be run from each stamper, the metalwork likely to be required would be one metal master, two mothers, and five stampers for each side, or 16 pieces total.

If tapes are to be made, there may or may not be a setup charge to cover making the duplicating master tapes. Some duplicators simply work the setup cost into the production unit price.

Similarly, pressing plants may either charge separately for the cost of test pressings or bury them into the production unit price. The reason for the charge is to offset setup cost, and most pressing plants will provide up to eight or ten pressings at no extra cost. In fact, they may have to run a dozen or more before the metalwork settles in and begins to produce representative pressings.

Many pressing plants include the cost of labels and plain white sleeves in the cost of the record. Ordered separately, labels and sleeves run a fraction of a cent each in large quantities and pennies each in small quantities.

Color separations are used only for full-color work. In one-, two-, or three-color work, the different colors are usually represented on overlays on the artwork. Each overlay, plus the basic pasteup, eventually becomes a litho negative after one or more intermediate film steps that are customarily included in the final negative charge. Photographs are rephotographed through a screen to make halftones, which are stripped into the litho negs. Brownlines and color keys are the composite proofs of final camera work for less-than-four-color and full-color respectively. The listed camera work is often done by the printing plant and is not always quoted separately.

Front and back surround (wrap) printing is priced individually because the front may be in full color while the back is printed in one, two, or three colors. In quantities of thousands, four-color printing is about twice as costly as one-color printing.

Sleeves for 45s are frequently printed, and it is not uncommon for LP sleeves to be imprinted with ads for other records a company has in release. Sleeve printing cost is added to the cost of the sleeve itself.

If the jacket of an album or a tape carton is to have a cut-out (sometimes done to make a label visible or to achieve an art effect), making a cutting die and the extra manufacturing step will entail added cost. Embossing is another optional expenditure.

Fancy four-color labels with photographic content are not included in basic record or tape costs. Unless the pressing plant is set up to handle four-color label printing, such labels will usually be better printed by an outside printer.

Converting, as mentioned earlier, is the process of gluing wraps onto basic jackets and can also include carton folding and gluing. Jacket varnishing, if ordered, is also done by the converter. Stuffing records into sleeves and jackets and putting tapes into boxes—also called collating—is a pressing plant or duplicator job that may be quoted separately, as is shrink-wrapping the assembled product.

Shipping costs can be incurred while moving tapes, artwork, printed materials, and finished product between various vendors and the record company's warehouse. How great these costs will be depends on the logistical arrangements with which the company is confronted. If all the work is done in the same city, vendor delivery is not uncommon.

Quotations should be obtained for all the individual cost items—e.g., pressings and jackets—and for turnkey manufacture by a single vendor so that the cost, quality, and logistical trade-offs can be evaluated sensibly. Quotations should be obtained for quantities of 1,000, 10,000, and 100,000 copies. The quote on 1,000 copies is needed because this is likely to be the quantity pressed to provide promotional copies to distributors, reviewers, and disc jockeys. The 10,000 and 100,000 quotes are needed because, statistically, the great majority of all records produced sell in numbers between these quantities and these quotes will be used for financial analyses.

FIGURE 11
Estimated Manufacturing Cost for 1,000 Albums

MANUFACTURING ESTIMATE WORKSHEET

Type of Record: ( ) Single (**X**) LP ( ) Cassette ( ) Cartridge   QUANTITY: *1,000*

	QUAN.	UNIT	UNIT COST	EXTENSION	TOTALS
ONE-TIME COSTS					
Records					
Metalwork	*2*	*PIECES*	*25*	*50*	
Test pressings	*1*	*SET*	*20*	*20*	
Tapes					
Duplicating setup/masters					
Packaging					
Color separations	*2*	*SETS*	*150*	*300*	
Color keys/proofs	*2*	*SETS*	*25*	*50*	
Halftones					
Stripping/etching					
Litho negatives					
Printing plates	*8*	*PIECES*	*12*	*96*	
Embossing, cutting dies					
			Total One Time Costs		*516.00*

VOLUME COSTS, for manufacturing quantity indicated above:

	QUAN.	UNIT	UNIT COST	EXTENSION	TOTALS
Record pressings		*EACH*	*.48*	*480*	
Cassettes, cartridges					
Labels		(*INCLUDED IN QUOTED PRESSING PRICE*			
Sleeves		(*INCLUDED IN QUOTED PRESSING PRICE*)			
Sleeve printing					
Print jacket fronts *4* colors		*M*	*65*	*65*	
Print jacket backs *4* colors		*M*	*65*	*65*	
Assemble (convert) jackets		*EACH*	*.10*	*100*	
Stuff jackets		*EACH*	*.03*	*30*	
Shrink-wrap album or tape		*EACH*	*.05*	*50*	
			Total Volume Costs		*790.00*
			TOTAL COSTS		*1,306.00*

FIGURE 12
Estimated Manufacturing Cost for 10,000 Albums
MANUFACTURING ESTIMATE WORKSHEET

Type of Record: ( ) Single (X) LP ( ) Cassette ( ) Cartridge   QUANTITY: _10 M_

	QUAN.	UNIT	UNIT COST	EXTENSION	TOTALS
ONE-TIME COSTS					
Records					
Metalwork	16	PIECES	20	320	
Test pressings	1	SET	20	20	
Tapes					
Duplicating setup/masters					
Packaging					
Color separations	2	SETS	150	300	
Color keys/proofs	2	SETS	25	50	
Halftones					
Stripping/etching					
Litho negatives					
Printing plates	8	PIECES	72	96	
Embossing, cutting dies					

Total One Time Costs **786.00**

VOLUME COSTS, for manufacturing quantity indicated above:

	QUAN.	UNIT	UNIT COST	EXTENSION	TOTALS
Record pressings		EACH	.47	4700	
Cassettes, cartridges					
Labels		(INCLUDED IN QUOTED PRESSING PRICE)			
Sleeves		(INCLUDED IN QUOTED PRESSING PRICE)			
Sleeve printing					
Print jacket fronts ____ colors		M	58	580	
Print jacket backs ____ colors		M	58	580	
Assemble (convert) jackets		EACH	.061	610	
Stuff jackets		EACH	.02	200	
Shrink-wrap album or tape		EACH	.02	200	

Total Volume Costs **6,870.00**

TOTAL COSTS **7,656.00**

FIGURE 13
Estimated Manufacturing Cost for 100,000 Albums

MANUFACTURING ESTIMATE WORKSHEET

Type of Record: ( ) Single (X) LP ( ) Cassette ( ) Cartridge   QUANTITY: **100 M**

	QUAN.	UNIT	UNIT COST	EXTENSION	TOTALS
ONE-TIME COSTS					
Records					
Metalwork	*ONE TIME COSTS IN THIS*				
Test pressings	*QUANTITY ARE SMALL*				
Tapes					
Duplicating setup/masters	*ENOUGH TO BE IGNORED,*				
Packaging					
Color separations	*FOR ESTIMATING PURPOSES*				
Color keys/proofs					
Halftones					
Stripping/etching					
Litho negatives					
Printing plates					
Embossing, cutting dies					
			Total One Time Costs		

VOLUME COSTS, for manufacturing quantity indicated above:

	QUAN.	UNIT	UNIT COST	EXTENSION	TOTALS
Record pressings		EACH	.44	44,000	
Cassettes, cartridges					
Labels	(INCLUDED IN PRESSING PRICE)				
Sleeves	(INCLUDED IN PRESSING PRICE)				
Sleeve printing					
Print jacket fronts **4** colors		M	50	5,000	
Print jacket backs **4** colors		M	50	5,000	
Assemble (convert) jackets		EACH	.05	5,000	
Stuff jackets		EACH	.02	2,000	
Shrink-wrap album or tape		EACH	.02	2,000	
			Total Volume Costs	**63,000**	
			TOTAL COSTS	**63,000**	

The quotations should be entered on manufacturing cost worksheets similar to those in Figures 11, 12, and 13. The figures on these worksheets are representative of quotes obtained in the Miami area in late 1979 and do not necessarily reflect the costs that would apply elsewhere in the country or at later dates, when inflation will doubtless cause them to rise. The cost figures are meant to be illustrative only, and a fresh set of real quotations should be obtained for every venture.

Most of the discussion in this book has been directed toward disc recordings because discs still account for the majority of all record sales (64 percent as compared with 25 percent for cartridges and 11 percent for cassettes in 1978). The dominant position of the disc is expected to continue in the future, but cassettes are rapidly displacing eight-track cartridges as the tape format of preference. It is an anomaly of the business that tape cassettes, which are obviously a far more complicated product than album discs, are cheaper to manufacture than most disc albums. The cassette itself costs more than the disc, but the jacket for an album costs more than the comparable box and packaging of a cassette because the cassette package uses less paper product, involves simpler assembly than a jacket, can be printed faster, and cannot contain the elaborate artwork of an album cover. In lots of 1,000, a forty-minute cassette that is boxed, labeled, and shrink-wrapped costs about 90¢, and its manufacture requires neither lacquer masters nor metalwork. However, because of the way the market works, cassettes are

TABLE 7

Quantity	Twelve-inch LP	Seven-inch Single
100	$2.50–$3.00	*
500	.48–.60	18–35¢
1,000	.48–.52	18–24¢
10,000	.46–.47	17.75–18.5¢

*Minimum print run for singles is 500.

produced and manufactured in addition to, not instead of, companion albums.

Disc costs, including one- or two-color labels, approximate the following figures. Plain white paper sleeves are included in the prices shown in Table 7.

Record Business
Economics

Thus far, only the costs and expenses of producing and manufacturing records have been discussed. The purpose of these outlays is to create a product that will sell and, ideally, produce enough income to recover all of the up-front outlay, pay the additional costs that are directly related to sales, and leave a large residue of profit. In this chapter, the income, cost, and profit interrelationships will be examined.

INCOME

How much a record sells for is determined by the manner in which it is sold.

If a high school band director produces a fund-raising album of the local high school band with the idea of selling the records to the kids and their doting parents, the target sales price will probably be arbitrarily set at $7 to $9, whatever the traffic will bear consistent with recovering costs, and whatever fund-raising excess (profit) was targeted. Sales might be made from door to door, through the school bookstore, and possibly by local merchants who would handle the records on a nonprofit basis as an accommodation to the charitable objectives for which the record was made. In a case like this, the whole selling price at the retail level might flow back to the school as income.

If the record is sold through normal channels of the record industry, however, the picture is different.

The company that produces and sells the record establishes the list price of the record. For an LP, cassette, or eight-track, the list price is typically $7.98, although budget albums are offered by some manufacturers at $6.98 or even $5.98 list price. In addition, some superstar records list for $8.98 or more. List price for 45 rpm singles is $1.49 with indications in late 1980 of an increase to $1.69 or even $1.79.

List prices are essentially meaningless from a consumer standpoint. Records listing at $7.98 usually sell in stores for $4.99 to $6.99, while 45s sell for $1.19 to $1.29.

Dealers (retailers) buy albums and tapes from distributors and rack jobbers at discounts of 46 percent to 50 percent of list price (e.g., between $4.00 and $4.30 for a $7.98 list item). The discount on 45s is lower, about 41 percent to 44 percent. This is of more or less academic interest to the manufacturer, because the manufacturer does not generally sell directly to dealers.

The company *does* sell to distributors and rack jobbers. The nominal wholesale price depends on whether the sale is made to the distribution subsidiary of a major record label (a "branch") or to an independent distributor/jobber (an "indie"). The company's price for a $7.98 list item is $3.47 to a branch or $3.60 to an indie. The price differential is presumably accounted for by the fact that the company assumes less credit risk with a branch than with an independent, that it is simpler to ship and invoice to the branches of a single company than to many separate independent distributors, and that the branch offers better promotion than an indie can. There is a great deal of disagreement within the industry as to whether the seeming advantages of a tie-in with a major label's branch distribution arrangements are beneficial for an independent label. The question is moot for most new independent labels anyhow because the major labels seek alliances only with other labels that have demonstrated potential for multimillion-dollar sales.

With either branch or independent distribution, the company will be under pressure to make special deals that reduce its revenue per record to below the nominal figures given above. Cash discounts for prompt payment will often be taken by distributors whether or not the payment has been made promptly. Whether or not a company accepts the loss of income or fights to recover it depends almost entirely on the strength of its products. It is common in the industry for manufacturers to prepay freight in whole or in part, or to "allow" freight, which means that the distributor pays the freight bill but deducts the paid amount from the amount invoiced by the manufacturer. Manufacturers may also offer bonus deals, in which an order for 100 records earns 5 additional free records for the distributor, for example.

For purposes of economic analysis, $3.35—about 42 percent of list—is a reasonable figure to use as a net-after-reductions amount for a record with a $7.98 list that is sold through independent distributors. The actual amount the company receives will depend on its total sales policy, and a different figure can be used for analysis if policy or prior experience with other records the company has produced makes some other amount more realistic.

COSTS

The costs of producing and manufacturing a hypothetical record album were given in the previous chapter. These figures will be used again for illustration in this chapter.

The production cost is a *fixed* cost; once a master tape is finished, any number of records from zero to millions can be manufactured from that tape without affecting what it cost to produce it.

Manufacturing costs are *semivariable*. It is not feasible to order pressings or tapes one at a time in response to orders received; these finished products have to be bought in quantity, both initially and on subsequent reorders. So for any specific quantity, such as 1,000 records, the cost is fixed. But for other quantities, the cost goes up and down in steps at points that reflect quantity breaks in manufacturers' quotations. Depending on the manufacturer, price breaks will occur for quantities of 500, 1,000, 10,000, 25,000, 50,000, and 100,000 units. By the time quantities reach 100,000 or so, all the manufacturing cost savings have been achieved so that further reductions in piece prices are minute.

Other costs vary directly with quantity, or nearly so. These *variable costs* include the royalties payable to producers and artists and for use of copyrighted music, and payments to the Musicians Performance and Phonograph Record trust funds (MPTF and PRTF). For each record sold—or, in the case of the copyright fees, distributed—fees will be payable. These variable costs can represent a significant percentage of total costs and have to be considered in working up profit or loss projections for a production venture.

The standard producer's agreement provides for the payment of royalties to the producer at a rate that is set at 3 to 4 percent of the list price of the record, or more for very "hot" producers. This rate depends on such negotiating factors as the producer's reputation, how urgently the company wants a particular producer, and, often, who has the better lawyer. Two clauses of the standard agreement reduce this nominal royalty rate.

The first reduces the royalty payable on the list price by some percentage that is referred to as a packaging allowance, which is commonly 10 to 20 percent of the list price. The theory behind this reduction is that the producer ordinarily doesn't have anything to do with the creation of the artwork or the design of the jackets or boxes that contain albums or tapes, and that, therefore, there is no justification for a producer to receive royalties on that portion of the finished product that isn't directly related to the musical production. There is some real validity to this theory, especially in light of the fact that the jacket may cost more to manufacture than the recording on some elaborate albums.

The second contract clause that cuts the effective royalty rate is one that harks back to the days when phonograph records were pressed from highly breakable shellac, and it provides that the producer will be paid the royalty on only 90 percent of the records sold. This is based on the theory that the record company will have to absorb the costs of records broken in shipment. While modern plastic records and tapes are far less susceptible to breakage than the old shellac pressings, the clause has lingered in the agreements as a matter of industry custom, not because there is any longer the rational basis for keeping it.

Without these clauses, a producer who had agreed to a 3½-percent rate on an album with a $7.98 list price would receive 27.9¢ per record sold. But, because of the way the clauses work in practice, the calculation of the producer's royalty in this case, assuming that the packaging allowance agreed to was 15 percent, would be as shown in Table 8.

TABLE 8

List price of the record	$7.98
Minus the packaging allowance (15%)	1.20
Equals the adjusted list price, for royalty purposes, of	6.78
Multiplied by the royalty rate factor (3.5%)	.035
Equals the per-record royalty amount	$0.2374

But, because the company will only be paying the almost 24¢ per record on 90 percent of the records it sells, the effective royalty cost on all records sold is 90 percent of the calculated amount, or 21.37¢ per record.

In this illustration, what appeared to be a 3½-percent royalty rate really turns out to be about 2.7 percent (the 21.37¢ divided by the $7.98 list price).

One other clause of the standard producer's agreement also affects the amount that the company will pay and the producer will receive in royalties. Again depending on the relative strengths and desires of the negotiating parties, the agreement may specify that the producer begins to earn royalties either from the first record sold or from the first record sold after the company has recovered all of its production costs. If the producer begins to earn royalties only after a sales floor established by production costs has been passed, both the company's costs and the producer's income are reduced further.

It is important to determine what downstream royalty costs are going to be during the budgeting process because royalties can account for a very significant portion of the cost of each completed record. Thus, they can have a real impact on the number of records that must be sold before profits begin to develop. Note, though, that any money advanced against earned royalties is deducted by the company before any cash payments are made to the producer.

The preceding calculation is predicated on the assumption that the standard form of agreement is used and that all sales are made in normal distribution in the United States. Royalties are usually reduced on foreign sales, on sales through record clubs, and on any other arrangement in which the company gets less than its normal income from sales. No royalty is payable on promotional records that are given away. The 21.37¢-per-record royalty figure will be used in illustrations that follow, but it is important to repeat that, as with all other cost examples in this book, a company should use its real costs based on its actual agreements, which do not necessarily have to follow standard forms and formats.

Artist royalty agreements follow a pattern similar to that for producers: list price is the base; packaging allowances and limitation to less than 100 percent of sales effectively reduce the base; the royalty is expressed as a percentage; and royalties are earned and/or payable only after some agreed floor has been passed. If musicians are royalty artists, the money they receive for their musical services is generally deducted from royalties earned before any payments become due.

Amounts payable as producer and artist royalties will be determined by the company's agreements with those people. The amounts payable to the Musician's Performance Trust Fund and the Phonograph Record Trust Fund are specified in the relevant agreements and are the same under each agreement. Again using the hypothetical album to illustrate the costs, reference to the agreements (Appendix C) shows that for a $7.98 list price, which exceeds $3.79, the contribution rate is 0.58 percent. This figure applies to the list price less the packaging allowance of 15 percent, or $6.78, so the contribution amount is 3.934¢ to each fund for each record sold.

The copyright royalties are payable on all records distributed, including records that are given away. So these royalties should be figured on 100 percent of the manufactured quantity. For illustration, it has been assumed that the record has eight tunes on it, none of which is longer than 5½ minutes, and that all are subject to copyright royalty payment at the statutory rate of 2.75¢ per tune. The resulting royalty is 22¢ per record.

PROJECTING PROFIT (LOSS)

Income and cost figures can now be used to determine whether or not the record venture is capable of being profitable and, for given sets of fixed, semivariable, and variable costs, how many records have to be sold to move from loss to profit.

Let us assume that the hypothetical record is going to be sold through normal distribution, that it lists for $7.98, and that the average income is about 42 percent of list. The revenue, then, for each record sold will be $3.35. But no matter how many records or tapes are manufactured, some number of these are going to be given away as promotional and review copies. If it is assumed that 10 percent of all records manufactured are given away free, all revenue has to be generated by the remaining 90 percent. On a projected profit (loss) statement (see Figure 14), the income for manufactured quantities of 1,000, 10,000, and 100,000 copies would be 90 percent of each of these quantities times $3.35.

The fixed production cost is taken from the financial budget column of the production budget worksheet (see Figure 10). But the $11,395 figure includes $2,000 that was advanced to the producer and will be recovered from earned royalties, so this amount should be deducted and the net production cost of $9,395 should be logged.

The semivariable manufacturing cost is taken from the manufacturing estimate worksheets that were prepared for the same quantities used for revenue projection (1,000, 10,000, and 100,000). Although income will be received for only 90 percent of these records, 100 percent of their cost will have to be borne.

The variable costs are shown in Figure 14. The 22¢-per-record fee for copyrighted music use is calculated for 100 percent of records manufactured. The payments to the two trust funds are calculated on 90 percent of the records manufactured, which is 100 percent of projected sales. Royalty amounts are calculated in accordance with the terms of the agreements made between the company, the producer, and the artists. In Figure 14, it has been assumed that only the producer is getting royalty compensation and that the amount will be based on the 3.5-percent rate discussed above. However, until the earned royalties exceed the amount advanced during the production phase, the company's royalty cost is the same as the amount advanced. So the amount entered is the larger figure of the amount earned and the amount advanced.

From the worksheet, it is obvious that a substantial loss would result if only 1,000 records were pressed and 900 were sold. If 9,000 copies are sold, the profit may represent an attractive return on invested capital, especially if all the records sell in a matter of weeks or months. At a quantity of 100,000, the gross profit becomes very large. Those readers who work out the profit projection on a million-album seller will see why people get into the record business despite the very

FIGURE 14
Projected Profit (Loss) Worksheet

MANUFACTURED QUANTITIES

	Amount Per Unit	1,000		10,000		100,000	
		Applicable Quantity	Amount	Applicable Quantity	Amount	Applicable Quantity	Amount
INCOME FROM SALES	$3.35	900	$3,015	9,000	$30,150	90,000	$301,500
COSTS/EXPENSES							
Fixed Production			9,395		9,395		9,395
Semi-Variable Manufacturing			1,306		7,656		63,000
Variable Copyright use	.22	1,000	220	10,000	2,200	100,000	22,000
MP trust fund	.03934	900	35	9,000	354	90,000	3,541
PR trust fund	.03934	900	35	9,000	354	90,000	3,541
Producer royalty*	.21366		2,000		2,000	90,000	19,230
Artists royalty*	—	—	—	—	—	—	—
Total Costs/Expenses			12,991		21,959		120,707
Projected Profit (Loss)			($9,976)		$ 8,191		$180,793

*Use the larger figure of royalties actually earned or advanced.

real risk that the record will be a dismal, loss-producing flop.

Other points disclosed by analysis of the various worksheets are as follows:

- Any mechanism that shifts cost from an out-of-pocket, up-front cost to a contingent cost that will be paid out of actual income cuts risk.
- Great care should be taken in deciding how many records to manufacture initially. The loss would be very large if the company pressed 100,000 records but only sold 10,000.
- Any mechanism that increases revenue per record without cutting sales will improve the bottom line. For some kinds of music (religious appears to be one kind) the added cost of television advertising and direct-mail sales may be much lower than the several dollars of additional revenue per record.
- The same desirable effect can be achieved by cutting cost. But the only places in which there is any real discretion for cost-cutting are in production (e.g., fewer musicians, less permissible studio time, a less costly one-color jacket, etc.), which can easily impact the eventual salability of the record; or in producer or artist royalties, which will inevitably transfer some cost out of deferred contingency back into up-front outlay.

A question that the company will want to answer for its own information and because investors are sure to ask it is, How many records must be sold to break even?

The equation for finding the break-even point is illustrated below.

$$\text{Breakeven Quantity} = \frac{F + SV}{P - V}$$

where

F is the fixed cost of production;
SV is the semivariable cost of manufacture;

P is the price of the record, net, that the company will get; and

V is the total of the variable costs for copyrighted music use, trust fund contributions, and royalties per record.

For the quantity of 100,000 records, the break-even point is

$$\frac{9{,}395 + 63{,}000}{3.35 - .51234} = 25{,}513 \text{ records}$$

The proof is as follows:

25,513 records @ $3.35 produces $85,466 in revenue. The costs are $9,395 + $63,000 + (25,513 times $0.51234), which also equals $85,466.

The equation will give incorrect answers when the costs exceed income, as in the case of 1,000 records pressed, and when earned royalties are lower than amounts advanced, as was the case for the 10,000 quantity. In the latter case, the error diminishes as the calculated break-even point approaches the point at which earned royalties equal advances. A correct answer can be obtained by simply adding up the total outlay for variable costs for the manufactured quantity, including the advanced amount ($4,554 in the case of 10,000) and dividing by the projected quantity to be sold (9,000) to arrive at an adjusted variable cost figure to plug into the equation. The correct quantity for breakeven in the case of 10,000 manufactured records turns out to be 6,061 records (vice 6,080 using the unadjusted variable costs).

REORDERS

If a record is selling well and the initial inventory is running low, a reorder should be considered. The profit on second and subsequent runs skyrockets because all the one-time production costs will have been absorbed in the company's books on the initial production quantity.

The tough question on reorders is: when and how many?

The answer depends on the results of some market research and analysis the company must do.

The first thing to do is to examine the incoming order flow from the time the record was released to the present date. The objective is to determine the trend line, to determine whether the sales trend at the present moment is upward, steady, or downward. Sales trends should be looked at on an overall basis *and* broken down by marketing regions (i.e., Northeast, Southeast, Northcentral, Midwest, West, etc.) because record acceptance is not always the same across the whole country.

Then look at returns. At the dealer and distributor levels, merchandisers will act fairly quickly to send records back when sales drop off, both to make room for faster-moving records and to obtain the monetary credits or refunds that make funds available for the purchase of hot sellers. Again examined on both national and regional bases, return figures matched against sales figures will indicate the probable market life of the record; the peak in returns will follow the peak in sales by roughly the same duration in all markets.

Next, contact the buyers at the distributing companies to which the company sells, and at any major retail record stores where the record is known to have been sold. Try to find out whether air play on the record is increasing, steady, or falling and what the merchandiser's near-term plan for the record is— a reorder, no action, or a return.

When evaluated, all of this information will indicate to the company whether it should manufacture more records and how large a production run it should commit itself to and at what point in time, taking manufacturing lead time into account. The idea is to reach the end-life of the record (negligible sales) with as few records left in inventory as possible, so that unsalable inventory does not eat up all the profits made on earlier sales. If the correct estimates have been made, the company will wind up filling its last order from Buffalo with the returns that came back from Los Angeles a few weeks earlier.

The information a company needs to gauge its production reruns is readily available if the record has hit the charts, but the odds against this happening are pretty high. Also, a record does not have to sell in chart-busting quantities to be very successful from an economic standpoint if the company was prudent in its production costs. When a record has not made the charts (such as those published each week in *Billboard*), then it will have to do its own market research as indicated above.

MINIMUM INVESTMENT RECORDS

For a church, a high school band, or any other organization that plans to make records with nonunion performers, the production costs may consist only of studio (or location recording) expenses, plus the cost of developing the artwork for the jacket. A number of pressing plants will deliver 1,000 finished albums in jackets with four-color fronts and one-color backs for $1,300 to $1,500, from finished master tape and camera-ready artwork. No trust-fund contributions will be made on such records, and even copyright royalties may be avoided by using either public domain music or music that has been composed specially for the recording and is made available free of royalty by the composer. But remember that if copyrighted music *is* used, a mechanical rights license must be secured and the required payments must be made to comply with federal law. This is true for all records, whether produced by amateurs or professionals.

It is possible to make acceptable, even excellent, recordings with nonprofessional equipment that is on the market today. Small groups whose music does not require the elaborate technical gimmickry available in professional studios may find it worthwhile to try to make a master tape using top-of-the-line audiophile or semiprofessional equipment. The tape machine should be equipped with two-track heads and should operate at 15 inches per second; the sacrifices in signal-to-noise and fidelity with ¼-track machines and 7½-inch speed are too great to accept, and not all mastering labs are even capable of mastering from such tapes. It is important to have top-quality microphones, and some familiarity and experience in mike selection and placement. Several mixers are available that accept four microphone inputs, have pan pots, and deliver two-channel output. These mixers have provisions for interconnection (paralleling buses) that permit two or more to be used in tandem to accommodate more microphones. An acoustically suitable recording location—low ambient noise and acceptable reverberation characteristics—will probably require a patient search and a lot of experimental recording, so what's really happening is that a group without a lot of money will have to invest its time instead to learn how to record with available equipment. Whether or not this makes sense depends on whether time or money is more important to the participants.

If an attempt is made to save on studio costs in this manner, it is very important to listen to the finished tape with an especially critical ear. Compare the final tape with records of music by groups that use similar instrumentation and perform similar music to see whether or not your finished tape stands up well when compared for sound quality. If it doesn't, don't waste money on mastering and pressings. Go to a studio and do a master that will compete in the marketplace.

Professional musicians who want to make a record for demonstration or sales purposes can legitimately reduce the actual cash required for production by banding together, forming a corporation, and agreeing that any amounts paid to them for musical services will be used to buy stock in the corporation. Payment will still be made to the union for Health and Welfare and Pension Fund contributions, and all payroll taxes will have to be paid, but the net earnings of the players can be plowed back to reduce the total cash requirement effectively. There is no reason why the plow-back cannot be made in the form of loans to the corporation so that the players ultimately receive the money for their services without payment of additional taxes (payroll taxes already having been paid). Later income can be used to finance additional records or can be distributed as dividends. This arrangement does not eliminate any of the artwork expenses, unless the artist can be persuaded to take stock for his or her services, too. Nor does it cut any part of the studio, manufacturing, or variable sales-related costs. However, it may reduce the up-front cash requirements enough to make it possible for a compatible group of artists to put out a record that they could not afford if they had to carry the full cost burden in cash. This approach also avoids the risks that union members run when they attempt to do bootleg records.

For our hypothetical record, the amount of cash needed in the financial column of the production budget would be reduced by about $2,600 (the gross payroll amount less withholding).

If a musical group gives a concert in a modern theater, there is a chance that the theater will have a very good sound system and a high-quality recorder. If the concert is carefully planned *and* the total sound system is capable of making good recordings *and* all musicians remember to stay on their microphones when they are playing, it is entirely possible that enough good material can be recorded to make an album without having to pay all the studio expenses. Or the group can pay for a studio remote unit, which will still cost less in most cases than for the same quantity of music recorded in a studio. One point is indisputable: music performed before a live and receptive audience is always freer, more spontaneous, and usually better, despite performer errors, than the same material recorded in the antiseptic environment of a studio. The problems are that useful studio tricks cannot be played, acoustics may not permit a really good recording, and an individual listener at home *will* hear those errors that are ephemeral events often unnoticed by live audiences.

Appendix A

Selection Timing Program for HP-97 Calculator

This program is designed to be used with Hewlett-Packard HP-97 calculators and can also be modified to work with HP-67 models.

To use:

1. Load program card.

2. Key in number of measures (bars) in song, excluding intros, segues, tags, etc., that are not played in every chorus. Press A.

3. Key in beats per measure. Press B. (Display will indicate product of steps 1 and 2.)

4. Key in *any two* of the following:

 • Tempo (beats per minute) and press C.

 • Desired number of choruses and decimal fraction of choruses (e.g., 4.5 for 4½ choruses). Press D.

 • Desired selection time in minutes and seconds. Press E.

5. Press a (gold key plus A). Printout is in this format:

   Number of measures in chorus
   Beats per measure
   Tempo, beats per minute
   Number of full choruses
   Number of extra bars
   Selection time in minutes and seconds

6. *Return to Step 2 for each new calculation; otherwise, errors will occur.*

001	*LBLA	21 11
002	DSF0	-63 00
003	CLRG	16-53
004	STOA	35 11
005	RTN	24
006	*LBLB	21 12
007	STOB	35 12
008	RCLA	36 11
009	X	-35
010	STO1	35 01
011	RTN	24
012	*LBLC	21 13
013	STOC	35 13
014	RTN	24
015	*LBLD	21 14
016	STOD	35 14
017	RTN	24
018	*LBLE	21 15
019	HMS+	16 36
020	STOE	35 15
021	RTN	24
022	*LBLa	21 16 11
023	RCLC	36 13
024	X=0?	16-43
025	GSBd	23 16 14
026	RCLD	36 14
027	X=0?	16-43
028	GSBc	23 16 13
029	RCLE	36 15
030	X=0?	16-43
031	GSBb	23 16 12
032	RCLA	36 11
033	PRTX	-14
034	RCLB	36 12
035	PRTX	-14
036	RCLC	36 13
037	PRTX	-14
038	RCLD	36 14
039	INT	16 34

040	PRTX	-14
041	RCLD	36 14
042	FRC	16 44
043	RCLA	36 11
044	X	-35
045	PRTX	-14
046	RCLE	36 15
047	→HMS	16 35
048	DSF2	-63 02
049	PRTX	-14
050	SFO	16-11
051	RTN	24
052	*LBLb	21 16 12
053	RCL1	36 01
054	RCLD	36 14
055	X	-35
056	RCLC	36 13
057	÷	-24
058	STOE	35 15
059	RTN	24
060	*LBLb	21 16 13
061	RCL1	36 01
062	RCLC	36 13
063	RCLE	36 15
064	X	-35
065	X÷Y	-41
066	÷	-24
067	STOD	35 14
068	RTN	24
069	*LBLd	21 16 14
070	RCL1	36 01
071	RCLD	36 14
072	X	-35
073	RCLE	36 15
074	÷	-24
075	STOC	35 13
076	RTN	24
077	R/S	51

141

Wage Scale Summary— AFM Nonsymphonic

AFM Wage Scales—Through 10/31/80 Nonsymphonic Recording Sessions

Type of Session	Session Duration	Usable Music	NUMBER OF SIDES ALLOWED New Music	Sweetening	BASIC SCALES Leader	Sidemar
Basic sessions, not during premium time						
Regular basic session	3 Hrs.	15 min.	No limit	4 sides	$274.43	$137.21
Overtime on regular basic session	½ Hr.	5 min.	No limit	1 side	91.48	45.74
Completion overtime, regular basic session	¼ Hr.	Permitted only to complete session			45.74	22.87
Typical basic sessions, including overtime;	3½ Hrs.	20 min.	No limit	5 sides	365.91	182.95
session may not extend into premium time	4 Hrs.	25 min.	No limit	6 sides	457.39	228.59
	4½ Hrs.	30 min.	No limit	7 sides	548.87	274.43
	5 Hrs.	35 min.	No limit	8 sides	640.35	320.17
Special session, 2-hour maximum duration						
Standard special session	1½ Hrs.	7½ min.	2 sides	Prohibited	181.12	90.56
Overtime on special session	½ Hr.	Permitted only to complete session			60.38	30.19
Overtime on special session	¼ Hr.	Permitted only to complete session			30.20	15.10

Basic sessions in premium time (weekdays after midnight, Saturday after 1 P.M., all day Sunday)
Multiply all above basic scales by 1.5 (150%)

Mixed basic sessions, partly in regular time, partly in premium time
Calculate regular and premium portions of session, add for total. Example: for basic session with 2 hrs. regular time and 1 hr. of premium time, divide regular basic session scale by 3 to get hourly rate. Total is 2 hrs. at this rate and 1 hr. at 150% of this rate.

Doubling: For each player who doubles, add 20% of basic scale applicable to the session in which doubling occurs for the first double and 15% of the basic scale for each additional double.
Tracking: Increase scale and doubling and cartage 100% for each tracking player for each tracking session.
Pension and Welfare Contribution (EPW): 10% of earnings (scale, doubling, tracking, but excluding cartage and Health and Welfare contributions).
Health and Welfare: $3.75 per musician per session (same for leader and sidemen).
Holiday Scale: Two times basic session and overtime rates.

Above basic scales increase 7% for 13-month period beginning November 1, 1980.

Appendix C

Phonograph Record Labor and Related Agreements

November 1979

Dated: New York, N.Y.

American Federation of Musicians of the
  United States and Canada
1500 Broadway
New York, N. Y. 10036

Gentlemen:

In consideration of the mutual covenants herein contained, of the promise of the undersigned company (herein called the "Company") fully and faithfully to perform each and every term, condition, and covenant on its part to be performed pursuant to the Phonograph Record Trust Agreement (November, 1979) and to the Phonograph Record Manufacturers' Special Payments Fund Agreement (November, 1979), both of which the Company is executing and delivering simultaneously herewith, and of other good and valuable considerations, the American Federation of Musicians of the United States and Canada (herein called the "Federation") has entered into this agreement with the Company setting forth the terms and conditions, including those set forth in Exhibits A, B, and C hereto attached, pursuant to which persons covered by this agreement may be employed by the Company in the recording of phonograph records.

1. This agreement shall cover and relate to members of the Federation wherever they shall perform, as employees, services for the Company as instrumental musicians or as leaders, contractors, copyists, orchestrators and arrangers of instrumental music (all of whom are collectively referred to as "musicians") in the recording of phonograph records, and to any other person employed as a musician in the recording of

145

phonograph records within the United States or Canada or a present territory or possession of either (herein called "Domestic Area"). This agreement shall also cover and relate to any resident of the Domestic Area engaged within the Domestic Area to perform such services outside the Domestic Area. It is further agreed that if a resident of the Domestic Area is engaged outside the Domestic Area to perform such services for the Company outside the Domestic Area, he shall, as a condition of employment, be and remain a member in good standing of the Federation. The Federation shall exercise full authority in order that its locals and members engaged in such activities shall do nothing in derogation of the terms and intent of this agreement.

2.   The Company shall not require, request, induce, or in any manner attempt to influence any person covered by this agreement to play, or perform for recordings, or render services pertaining thereto, except as permitted by this agreement.

3.   For the services rendered by the persons covered by this agreement in the making of recordings, the Company shall pay at least Federation scale as provided in Exhibit "A". The Company shall fully and faithfully perform the terms and conditions of its individual agreements with such persons. In addition, the persons covered by this agreement in the making of recordings shall be entitled to their respective portions of the musicians' share of the Fund under Exhibit "C" hereto.

4.   Following the execution of this agreement, the Company shall promptly furnish to the Federation, upon request, a copy of all of the Company's record catalogs, and a schedule of its manufacturer's suggested retail prices for each record in its catalogs, and thereafter from time to time, a schedule listing all amendments and additions thereto, as and when established.

5.   At the end of each month the Company shall advise the Federation of all recordings released by the Company during such month, of the serial or other number thereof, and of any additional information in connection with any such recording which the Federation may reasonably require. Upon request by the Federation, the Company shall promptly furnish to it a

copy of any such recording. The Company shall respond promptly to reasonable requests by the Federation for information relating to the Company's performance of the terms and conditions of this agreement and of any and all individual agreements with persons covered by this agreement.

If the Company shall sell, assign, lease, license or otherwise transfer title to any other person, any master record (as defined in Addendum A to the Phonograph Record Manufacturers' Special Payments Fund Agreement) produced under this agreement (or its predecessors if such transaction occurs after November 1, 1979) for the purpose of allowing such other person to manufacture phonograph records for sale, the Company shall report to the Federation the name and address of each such purchaser, assignee, lessee, licensee, or transferee and shall identify the record involved. The Company shall report all such transactions monthly.

6.   Except as otherwise specifically provided in Exhibit A hereto and without regard to the duration of this agreement, the Company shall not dub, re-record, or re-transcribe (herein called "dub") any recordings containing performances by persons covered by any Phonograph Record Labor Agreement with the Federation since January 1954 and rendered during the term of any such agreements, provided that during the term of this agreement the Company may dub if it shall first give notice of its intention so to do to the Office of the President of the Federation. In the event of such dubbing the Company shall pay to all persons covered by this agreement as additional compensation for the rendition of such original performances an amount equal to the scale for such new use and shall also make any and all additional payments applicable to such new use. For the purposes of this agreement, the term "dub" shall not include the use of all of the contents of any master, matrix, mother, stamper, or similar device from which records can be produced (herein called "master record") for the production of new phonograph records (1) which in their entirety only contain the identical content of the records originally produced from such master records, and (2) which are intended to be used for the same purposes to which the records originally produced from such master record were principally devoted.

— 3 —

7. Persons covered by this agreement shall not make or be required to make phonograph records containing commercial advertisements, or any phonograph records to be used by or for performers as accompaniment for or in connection with their live performances. The Company shall not furnish orchestra tracks without vocals to artists or any other person without prior approval of the Federation.

8. The Company shall not make recordings of instrumental music, or permit the use of its facilities or otherwise give aid and assistance in recording instrumental music, for or on account of any other person, firm or corporation unless authorized in writing by the Federation, which authorization shall not unreasonably be withheld.

9. The Company agrees not to make recordings of any radio or television programs, containing the services of persons covered by Phonograph Record Labor Agreement (November, 1979), off-the-line or off-the-air, without first obtaining written permission from the Office of the President of the Federation, except that no such permission shall be necessary in instances where such recordings are (a) for reference or file purposes, or (b) for the purpose of making delayed broadcast transcriptions which have been authorized in writing by the Federation.

The Federation agrees that in all cases it will not unreasonably withhold permission to make such off-the-air or off-the-line recordings, and that in such other instances where granted, permission shall be given on payment of the phonograph record scale, and of any and all additional payments applicable to such new use. This agreement shall not in any way modify any obligation independent of this agreement which the Company may be under to obtain other individual approvals as may be necessary in connection with such off-the-line or off-the-air recordings.

10. The Company hereby recognizes the Federation as the exclusive bargaining representative of persons covered by paragraph 1 of this agreement.

11. The following provisions contained in this paragraph "11" shall apply only to recording services to be rendered hereunder in Canada where not prohibited by applicable law.

— 4 —

(a) Only the services of members in good standing of the American Federation of Musicians of the United States and Canada shall be used for the performance of all instrumental music, and in the copying, orchestrating or arranging of such music, in recording phonograph records, and, in the employment of persons who are eligible for membership in the Federation, only such persons as shall be members thereof in good standing shall be so employed.

(b) As the musicians referred to or engaged under the stipulations of this contract are members of the American Federation of Musicians of the United States and Canada, nothing in this contract shall ever be construed so as to interfere with any obligation which they may owe to the American Federation of Musicians of the United States and Canada as members thereof.

(c) (1) Any employee(s) covered by this Agreement whose services hereunder are prevented, suspended, or stopped by reason of any lawful primary strike, ban, or unfair list of the Federations, shall, for the duration of such lawful primary strike, ban, or unfair list, and for no longer than the duration thereof: (A) be free to suspend the performance of services hereunder; and (B) be free to perform services in other employment of the same or similar character, or otherwise, for other employers, or persons, firms or corporations, without any restraint, hinderance, penalty, obligation, or liability whatever, any other provision of this Agreement to the contrary notwithstanding; provided, however that upon the cessation of such lawful primary strike, ban, or unfair list, any and all such contractual obligations owed by employees covered by this Agreement to the Company, which were suspended by reason of such strike, ban, or unfair list, shall immediately be revived and shall be in full force and effect.

(2) It shall not be a violation of this Agreement, nor cause for disciplinary action, if a musician covered by this Agreement refuses to cross or to work behind a lawful primary picket line of the Federation which has been posted by the Federation in connection with a dispute arising under this Agreement, including a lawful primary picket line of the

— 5 —

Federation at the Employer's place of business or at a place of business to which a musician(s) covered by this Agreement is sent by the Employer to perform services hereunder.

12. The following provisions of this paragraph "12" shall apply to recording services rendered in the United States, its territories and possessions.

(a) It shall be a condition of employment that all employees of the employer covered by this labor agreement who are members of the union in good standing on the execution date of this union security agreement shall remain members in good standing and those who are not members on the execution date of this union security agreement shall on the 30th day following said execution date become and remain members in good standing in the union. It shall also be a condition of employment that all employees covered by this labor agreement and hired on or after said execution date shall on the 30th day following the beginning of such employment become and remain members in good standing in the Federation.

(b) As to the musicians referred to or engaged under the stipulations of this contract who are members of the American Federation of Musicians of the United States and Canada, and to the extent to which the inclusion and enforcement of this paragraph is not prohibited by any presently existing and valid law, nothing in this contract shall ever be construed so as to interfere with any obligation which they may owe to the American Federation of Musicians of the United States and Canada as members thereof.

(c) (1) Any employee(s) covered by this Agreement whose services hereunder are prevented, suspended, or stopped by reason of any lawful primary strike, ban, or unfair list of the Federation, shall, for the duration of such lawful primary strike, ban, or unfair list, and for no longer than the duration thereof: (A) be free to suspend the performance of services hereunder; and (B) be free to perform services in other employment of the same or similar character, or otherwise, for other employers, or persons, firms, or corporations, without any restraint, hinderance, penalty, obligation, or liability whatever, any other provision of this Agreement to the contrary notwithstanding; provided, however, that upon the cessation of such lawful primary strike, ban, or unfair list, any and all such contractual objigations owed by employees covered by this Agreement to the Company, which were suspended by reason of such strike, ban, or unfair list, shall immediately be revived and shall be in full force and effect.

(2) It shall not be a violation of this Agreement, nor cause for disciplinary action, if a musician covered by this Agreement refuses to cross or to work behind a lawful primary picket line of the Federation which has been posted by the Federation in connection with a dispute arising under this Agreement, including a lawful primary picket line of the Federation at the Employer's place of business or at a place of business to which a musician(s) covered by this Agreement is sent by the Employer to perform services hereunder.

13.   (a) All present provisions of the Federation's Constitution and By-Laws are made part of this agreement to the extent to which their inclusion and enforcement are not prohibited by any applicable law. No changes therein made during the term of this agreement shall be effective to contravene any of the provisions hereof.

(b) The following provision shall be included in, and whether or not so included, shall be deemed part of all contracts calling for recording services between the Company and persons covered by this agreement:

"This contract shall become effective unless it is disapproved by the International Executive Board of the American Federation of Musicians of the United States and Canada, or a duly authorized agent thereof, within 30 working days after it is submitted to the International Executive Board. The parties acknowledge that this provision is not intended to provide a device for the parties hereto to avoid their obligations."

14.   The duly authorized representatives of the Federation and also of the local (affiliated with the Federation), upon

presentation of proper identification to the Company, shall each be granted access to the studio or other place where services are being performed hereunder. Each shall be permitted to visit that place during working hours for the proper conduct of the business of the Federation or such local, respectively.

15. (a) The Company agrees that it shall furnish to the Federation, simultaneously with its delivery thereof to the Trustee and to the Administrator named in the Special Payments Fund Agreement (November, 1979) copies of any and all statements submitted to the Trustee and to the Administrator.

(b) The Company agrees that the Federation shall have the right from time to time, without limitation to the duration of this agreement, and at all reasonable times during business hours, to have the Federation's duly authorized agents examine and audit the Company's records and accounts concerning all transactions involving the Company's sale of phonograph records which it shall keep pursuant to said Trust Agreements and to said Special Payments Fund Agreements and such other records and accounts as may be necessary; such examination and audit to be made for the purpose of the Federation's verifying any statements made by the Company pursuant to said agreements, during a period not exceeding four (4) years preceding such examination, and of determining the amount of payments due by it thereunder. It is agreed that the four (4) year period provided herein shall not effect the operation of the applicable statute of limitations. The Company agrees to afford all necessary facilities to such authorized agents to make such examination and audit and to make extracts and excerpts from said records and accounts as may be necessary or proper according to approved and recognized accounting practices. Examinations and audits made pursuant hereto shall be coordinated, to the extent practicable, with examinations and audits made under the aforesaid Trust Agreements and Special Payments Fund Agreements so that inconvenience to the Company may be minimized.

16. If during the term hereof, the Federation shall enter into an agreement with any phonograph record company upon terms more favorable than or different from those contained in

this agreement, the Company shall have the right at its option to cause this agreement to be conformed therewith, provided, however, that no such right shall come into being by reason of the compromise of any claim against any recording company by reason of the insolvency, bankruptcy or other financial difficulty of such company.

17.   The Company shall not produce any phonograph record from recorded music acquired or taken from or licensed by any other person, firm or corporation, in the making of which there was utilized instrumental music recorded within the Domestic Area or by a person who, at the time of the recording resided within the Domestic Area, unless the total cost to the person, firm or corporation which produced the recorded music with respect to the scale of wages and fringe benefits paid to the musicians was at least equal to what the cost would have been under the Phonograph Record Labor Agreement of the Federation which was in effect at the time the recorded music was produced; provided, however, that if such music was recorded outside of the Domestic Area, no payment need be made pursuant to this paragraph if the music was acquired, taken or licensed before January 1, 1964.

The Company may satisfy its obligation under this paragraph by incorporating in an agreement under which it acquires the right to use recorded music, a representation and warranty by the seller or licensor (which the Company shall guarantee if the seller or licensor was not a party to a Phonograph Record Labor Agreement with the Federation when the recording was made) that such recorded music does not come within the terms of this paragraph or that the requirements of this paragraph have been satisfied and a statement that such representation and warranty was included for the benefit of the Federation (among others) and may be enforced by the Federation or by such person or persons as it may designate. Upon request, a signed copy of such agreement shall be furnished to the Federation. No rights or privileges existing or accrued between January 1, 1959 and October 31, 1979, shall be deemed waived by reason of the provisions of this paragraph. (Numbered "18" in some prior agreements.)

— 9 —

18. Except as specifically provided in paragraphs 6, 8, 9 and 17, nothing contained in this agreement is intended to or shall be deemed to relate to the rendition of services or to dubbing in connection with the production of devices other than phonograph records as such devices are presently known.

19. (a) This Agreement shall be personal to the Company and shall not be transferable or assignable, by operation of law or otherwise, without the written consent of the Federation, which consent shall not unreasonably be withheld.

(b) Without the written consent of the Federation, which consent shall not unreasonably be withheld, the Company shall not transfer or assign any individual contract (or part thereof) for the performance of services by a person(s) covered by this Agreement, or give another person control over such contract of such services. Provided, however, that consent by the Federation shall not be required if the person to whom such individual contract (or part thereof) is transferred or assigned or to whom such control is given: (1) is at the time of such transfer, or agrees to become a party to this Agreement; or (2) will incur total labor costs (for wages and fringe benefits) with respect to the services covered by such individual contract, which are at least equal to the total labor costs (for wages and fringe benefits) which would be incurred under the scale of wages and fringe benefits provided for under this Agreement.

(c) Nevertheless, if the provisions of Paragraphs (a) or (b) of this Section 19 are violated, and services are thereafter performed by such individual(s), the obligations and duties imposed by this Agreement shall be binding upon the transferee or assignee with respect to such individual(s).

(d) The obligations imposed by this Agreement upon the Company, shall be binding upon the Company, and to the extent permitted by applicable law, upon such of its subsidiaries as are engaged in the production of phonograph records in the Domestic Area.

(e) To the extent permitted by applicable law, the Federation, at its option, may, upon 90 days written notice to both the transferee and the transferror, terminate this Agreement at any time after a transfer of any controlling interest in the Company.

20.   The Company will simultaneously herewith execute and deliver the Phonograph Record Manufacturers' Special Payments Fund Agreement in the form attached hereto as Exhibit C, or in such other form or forms, with such other terms and conditions, as the Company and the Federation may hereafter and from time to time agree on, and such agreement when so modified or changed by the Company and the Federation shall be binding upon the Administrator under said Special Payments Fund Agreement and he shall execute a counterpart of such changed or modified Special Payments Fund Agreement.

21.   The parties reaffirm their long established and prevailing policy and practice that every person shall have an opportunity to obtain employment without discrimination because of race, creed, color, sex, or national origin. In furtherance of such policy and practice the parties agree that in the hiring of employees for the performance of work under this Agreement neither the Company nor the Federation shall discriminate by reason of race, creed, color, sex, national origin or union or non-union membership against any person who is qualified and available to perform the work to which the employment relates.

22.   A joint committee of representatives of Industry and the Federation will be established for the purpose of addressing problems of mutual concern which may arise under this Agreement.

23.   This Agreement shall be effective for the period from November 1, 1979 to and including November 30, 1981.

Your signature in the space provided below will constitute this a binding agreement between you and us.

Very truly yours,

_____

Exact Legal Full Name of Company

By:_____

Signature of Company's Authorized Officer or Agent

_____

Print Name and Title of Company's Officer or Agent

_____

Company's Address

EXHIBIT A

I

MINIMUM WAGES AND OTHER WORKING CONDITIONS

INSTRUMENTALISTS, LEADERS, CONTRACTORS

Instrumentalists, leaders and contractors shall be paid not less than the rates set forth below and the conditions set forth shall apply:

A. *In the case of phonograph records other than those recorded by symphonic orchestras:*

(1) There shall be a minimum call Basic Regular Session of three hours during which there may be recorded not more than 15 minutes of recorded music; provided, however, that in a session where sweetening (i.e., instrumental performances added to music recorded at a previous session) is performed not more than 4 single record sides or 4 segments of long play or extended play records may be sweetened. Subsequent continuous regular sessions may be arranged if the musicians have been notified and consented thereto before the end of the preceding session and if there is a 30 minute rest period between the two sessions.

(2) There shall be a minimum call Special Session of 1½ hours during which there may be recorded not more than two sides containing not more than 7½ minutes of recorded music. Unless the musicians are notified when they are engaged that the call is for a Special Session, it shall be deemed to be a Regular Session. In a Special Session there may be no sweetening. The maximum overtime in a Special Session shall be ½ hour, paid for in quarter hour units, which can only be used to complete the one or two sides of the original Special Session.

(3) Overtime for Regular Sessions shall be paid for in units of one-half hour or final fraction thereof. During the one unit of overtime for a Regular Session there may be recorded or completed not more than five minutes of recorded music; provided however, that in a unit where sweetening is performed, not more than one single record side or one segment of a long play or extended play record may be sweetened.

— 13 —

Notwithstanding the above, overtime may be paid for in one one-quarter hour unit if such time is used only to complete the music recorded within the permissible limits of the foregoing provisions.

(4) There shall be two 10 minute rest periods during each basic Regular Session and one 10 minute rest period during each Basic Special Session. No rest period shall commence sooner than 30 minutes following the beginning of any session call provided that all musicians who are scheduled to participate in the call are present at the commencement of the call. In addition, there shall be one 5 minute rest period during each hour of overtime, it being understood that such a rest period need not be called during the first half-hour of overtime.

(5) The minimum pay, per sideman, shall be as follows:

	Basic Rate	Overtime Rate ½ Hour Unit	Overtime Rate ¼ Hour Unit
Effective November 1, 1979			
Regular Session	$137.21	$45.74	$22.87
Special Session	90.56	30.19	15.10
Effective November 1, 1980			
Regular Session	$146.82	$48.94	$24.47
Special Session	96.90	32.30	16.15

NOTE: See A (2) and (3) for overtime restrictions.

(6) *Health and Welfare Fund Contributions*
   (Non-Symphonic):

The Company will contribute to any existing lawful Health and Welfare Fund of any Federation Local and commencing thirty days after notice in writing to any such lawful Fund as may be established hereafter by any other Federation Local, the sum of $3.75 for each original service on non-symphonic records performed within the jurisdiction of such Federation Local by each musician covered by this agreement.

With respect to any such original service performed within the jurisdiction of a Federation Local where no such Fund is established, the Company shall pay to each such musician said sum of $3.75.

— 14 —

No such Health and Welfare Fund contribution whether paid to any Fund or paid directly to a musician shall be the basis for computing the applicable AFM-EPW contribution or any other payments under this agreement such as doubling, overtime, premium time pay, etc.

(7) *Premium Rates* (Non-Symphonic):

(a) One and one-half (1½) times the basic session and over-time rates shall be paid for all hours of recording, (i) between midnight and 8:00 A.M., (ii) after 1:00 P.M. on Saturdays and (iii) on Sundays.

(b) Two times the basic session and overtime rates shall be paid for all hours of recording on any of the following holidays:

In the United States

New Year's Day	Labor Day
Washington's Birthday	Thanksgiving
Memorial Day	Christmas
Independence Day	

In Canada

New Year's Day	Dominion Day
Good Friday	Labour Day
Easter Monday	Thanksgiving
Victoria Day	Christmas

Each of these holidays shall be observed on the day on which it is observed by employees of the United States Government or of the Government of Canada.

(c) The premium rates provided for in this paragraph numbered 7 shall not apply to show album recordings on Saturdays and Sundays nor to location recordings made on location during public performance, nor to Royalty Artists as defined in Paragraph L. (f) (i) (Page 26) unless such an artist is performing in a session scheduled at the express request of the Company.

B. *In the case of phonograph records recorded by symphonic orchestras:*

(1) There shall be a minimum call Basic Session of 3 hours or 4 hours, determined in accordance with sub-paragraph (3)

— 15 —

below, during which the playing time shall not exceed an average of 40 minutes for each hour with an average rest period of 20 minutes for each hour. The intermission shall be divided by the contractor so as not to interrupt proper recording of symphonic works subject to (4) below. The wages and working conditions for symphonic recordings are predicated upon the fact that the orchestra will have had rehearsed numbers in its repertoire and therefore will need no rehearsals for recordings.

(2) The basic session shall be three hours unless the company by notice prior to any session elects a four-hour basic session, provided that no more than one such four-hour session may be called for any day. Unless such notice is given the session shall be deemed to be a three-hour session. No more than an average of seven and one-half minutes of finished recorded music may be made from each one-half hour segment of a recording session (including all overtime periods), and for this purpose multiple sessions devoted to the same composition shall be considered one session, so that the seven and one-half minutes of finished recorded music may be averaged out of each such session.

(3) Overtime shall be paid for in units of one-half hour or final fraction thereof. During one unit of overtime, the playing time shall not exceed 20 minutes.

Notwithstanding the above, overtime may be paid for one one-quarter hour unit if such time is used only to complete the music recorded within the permissible limits of the foregoing provisions.

(4) No musician shall be required to work for more than 60 consecutive minutes without a rest period of at least 10 minutes.

(5) All members of the symphony orchestra, whether called to the engagement or not, shall be paid for at least the first two (2) hours of the basic session call $96.96 effective 11-1-79 and $103.75 effective 11-1-80 and shall not be called or required to attend if they are not scheduled to perform.

(6) The minimum pay, per sideman, for a basic session (Column A or B), for a unit of regular overtime before the

completion of six (6) hours of work in any day (Column C or E—1½ time) and for a unit of premium overtime after the completion of six (6) hours of work in any day (Column D—double time), shall be as follows:

Effective November 1, 1979:

A	B	C ½-Hour Unit of "Regular Overtime" (1½ time pay)	D ½-Hour Unit of "Premium Overtime" (double time)	E ¼-Hour Unit of "Regular Overtime" (1½ time pay)
"Basic Session Rate" 3 Hour Session	"Basic Session Rate" 4 Hour Session			
$145.44	$193.92	$36.36	$48.48	$18.18

Effective November 1, 1980:

$155.62	$207.50	$38.90	$51.87	$19.45

(7) *Premium Rates* (Symphonic):

With respect to sessions (other than location recordings made during public performance) held between (i) midnight and 8:00 A. M.

(i) On Saturdays or Sundays if either day is a regular day off by contract or custom (which shall not be changed during the term of this agreement), or

(ii) On any of the holidays listed below, one and one-half (1½) times the basic session rate shall be paid for the first two hours, one and one-half (1½) times the regular overtime rate shall be paid in respect of the next four (4) hours and one and one-half (1½) times the premium overtime rate shall be paid in respect of all recording time in excess of six (6) hours:

In the United States

New Year's Day
Washington's Birthday
Memorial Day
Independence Day

Labor Day
Thanksgiving
Christmas

— 17 —

In Canada

New Year's Day	Dominion Day
Good Friday	Labour Day
Easter Monday	Thanksgiving
Victoria Day	Christmas

Each of these holidays shall be observed on the day on which it is observed by employees of the United States Government or of the Government of Canada.

(8) *Location Recordings*

The following provisions apply to the recording of complete operas, symphonies, and similar works performed by opera and symphonic orchestras during public performances.

There is no limit on the number of performances of a work that may be recorded during a season. The orchestra shall be notified of the work to be recorded in advance of the recording and only that work may be recorded. The first recording session shall trigger a guarantee payment for one 3-hour session at the "basic session rate." Upon release, the complete work shall be paid for at the "basic session rate" on the basis of one session hour for each 10 minutes of finished product, against which the guarantee payment may be credited. (For example, a 45-minute work equates to 4½ hours, computed at straight time rates; a 25-minute work would be covered by the 3-hour guarantee.)

The provisions of paragraph (7) hereof do not apply to recordings made under this paragraph (8).

(9) *Health and Welfare Fund Contributions* (Symphonic—"Extra" Musicians)

Extra musicians, if not covered by an applicable Orchestra Health and Welfare Plan, shall be treated in accordance with the applicable provisions of I A (6) on page 14 in the case of instrumentalists, or II D on page 34 in the case of copyists.

C. *Chamber Music*

In lieu of the provisions of Paragraph B above, the Company may record chamber music under the following terms and conditions:

(a) The producer shall give the Federation 4-weeks advance notice of intent to record under this provision and should the Federation claim that this provision does not apply, it shall inform the producer of that position with its reasons therefor.

(b) There shall be a 4 hour basic session rate of $151.20 ($161.78 effective November 1, 1980), with overtime at time and one half, in half hour segments.

(c) 45-minutes of finished music may be taken from a 4-hour session.

(d) One 15-minute rest period per hour.

(e) Non-symphonic conditions and benefits apply unless otherwise provided.

(f) Neither the recording nor its package may claim or imply that the chamber group is associated with a parent symphony orchestra except where the recorded music is performed by no more than 9 players not playing multiple parts. This restriction does not preclude biographical sketches which identify the players as members of a symphony orchestra.

(g) This provision shall not be used

  i. to record compositions requiring more than 24 players or compositions of less than 5 minutes duration without prior Federation approval;

  ii. for transferring from one medium to another (i.e., for production of sound track albums).

D. *Leaders and Contractors*

The leader and contractor shall receive not less than double the applicable sideman's scale, but in any event, the scale for any one person shall not exceed double sideman's scale.

If twelve or more sidemen are employed for any session, a contractor shall be employed in respect of said session. The contractor shall be in attendance throughout the session for which he is employed. The contractor may be one of the sidemen at the session.

At each session one person shall be designated as leader but in the event only one person performs the musical service at a session, only that person can be designated as leader.

E. *Dismissal and overtime*

Musicians shall be dismissed upon completion of performances for which they have been engaged whether or not the full session has expired. Musicians may record at any time during the session for which they have been engaged.

No musician shall be required to remain longer than one half hour overtime unless a longer time requirement was specified at the time he accepted the engagement.

F. *Advance notice of sessions and contract information*

When the company has prior knowledge of a session it will give advance notice to the appropriate Federation Local.

Where the Company employs an independent producer, the Company shall seek to include in the contract with such producer a provision which obligates such producer to notify the appropriate Federation Local in advance of recording sessions called by the producer. The Company will provide to the Federation a list of such producers who do not agree to include such provision in their contracts with the Company.

If a session is called to add to existing musical tracks the Company will, at the request of the Local having jurisdiction in the area where the session is called, provide the Local with dates, places and contract numbers of prior sessions on the basis of Form B contracts in the Company's files.

The Company will notify the Federation and the appropriate Local of any change in title of a song listed on a Form B contract.

The Company shall submit a listing to the Federation of non-signatory independent producers with their names, addresses and telephone numbers. Standby calls shall be prohibited.

The Company, or its authorized agent, shall announce the name of the signatory employer at the time of the calling of the session.

G. *Session Calls and Cancellation*

A session, once called, shall not be cancelled, postponed, or otherwise rescheduled less than 7 days prior to the date of the session. In the event of an emergency, a session may be cancelled, postponed or otherwise rescheduled upon shorter notice with the consent of the office of the Federation President.

H. *Doubling*

(1) When a musician plays one or more doubles during any session or during any unit of overtime or both, he shall be paid an additional 20% of the applicable session rate and the overtime related thereto for the first double and an additional 15% of such rate for each double thereafter.

(2) Instruments within the following respective groups are not construed as doubling:

(a) Piano and celeste (when furnished).

(b) Drummer's standard outfit consisting of bass drum, snare drum, cymbals, gongs, piatti, small traps, and tom toms when used as part of a standard outfit.

(c) Tympani.

(d) Mallet instruments: xylophone, bells and marimbas.

(e) Latin rhythm instruments: Any Latin instrument when used in less than eight bars in connection with any other instrument or used not in a rhythm pattern shall not in any event be a doubling instrument.

(3) Fretted instruments: Performance on more than two instruments within group (a) below or performance on any one instrument in group (a) together with any one instrument in group (b) below shall be treated as doubling. Performance of two or more instruments within group (b) below shall be treated as doubling:

(a) 6-String rhythm guitar
    6-String electric guitar

— 21 —

"Combo" guitar (rhythm and electric combined)
6-String (steel) round hole guitar
6-String (nylon) classic guitar
12-String acoustic guitar
12-String electric guitar

(b) 6-String bass guitar
Tenor banjo
Plectrum
5-String banjo
Mandolin
Ukulele
Sitar

(4) Electronic devices: If an electronic device (e.g. multiplex, divider, maestro, multiplier of octaves) is used to simulate sounds of instruments in addition to the normal sound of the instrument to which such electronic device is attached or applied, such use of the electronic device shall be treated as a double.

(5) A special fee of $5 shall be paid for each additional instrument requiring a doubling fee which the musician is directed to bring to the engagement if such instrument is not actually used.

I. *Location recordings* (Non-Symphonic)

The Company shall give prior notice to the Office of the Federation President and to the Local of the Federation involved prior to making any recording on location during public performance. Location recording work shall be paid for at the rate of one basic session for each day of recording (from noon to the following noon). During any such day, no more than a total of three hours of performance shall be recorded. If more than fifteen minutes of recorded music is released for sale from each such three hours of recorded performance, the Company shall make additional payments equal to the regular hourly rate of pay for each additional five minutes of recorded music (or fraction thereof) released for sale. The Company agrees to send to the Office of the Federation President at the time of first release a copy of every album resulting from any such location recording.

The Company shall list the musical selections recorded at a location session from the tapes delivered to the Company by the producer and shall furnish to the Federation a copy of such list.

When a recording on location is released, the Company shall notify the orchestrators, arrangers and copyists involved in the tunes released in advance of such release so that they may submit their invoices for payment.

J. *Cartage*

The Company shall pay for actual cartage at the following rate, except that in lieu thereof the Company shall pay the submitted bills of a public carrier when any of these instruments are delivered by such carrier and such public carrier shall be used when it is the only practicable method of transportation.

Harp—$26 ($28 effective November 1, 1980); Accordion, String Bass, Tuba, Drums, all Amplifiers, Baritone Saxophone, Bass Saxophone, Cello, Contrabassoon, Contra Bass Clarinet—$6 each.

K. *Payment*

(1) Payment to instrumental musicians

The Company shall make the payments set forth in Exhibit A to each leader, contractor, and sideman employed at a recording session, through such agency or agencies of the Federation as may be designated from time to time by the Federation, within 15 days (excluding Saturdays, Sundays and holidays) after the date of receipt from the contractor, if any, or the leader of the recording session of a completed Form B and all completed W-4 forms.

(2) Payment to arrangers, orchestrators, or copyists

The Company shall make payment to arrangers, orchestrators, or copyists for work performed under the terms of this agreement, through such agency or agencies of the Federation as may be designated from time to time by the Federation, within 15 days (excluding Saturdays, Sundays, and holidays) after the date of receipt of their completed billings and all necessary and completed W-4 forms.

(3) Health and Welfare payments

The Company shall make health, welfare and pension fund contributions as set forth in Exhibit A to instrumental musicians at the same time the Company pays the musicians for the sessions.

(4) The contract Form B number shall be on or accompany the payment statements.

(5) (a) A penalty of 5% of the above-mentioned amount due and unpaid if the delinquent payment is made within 5 days (excluding Saturday, Sunday and holidays) after payment was due.

(b) A penalty of 7½% of the above-mentioned amount due and unpaid (excluding the penalty in 5a above) if the delinquent payment is made between the 6th and 10th business days (excluding Saturday, Sunday and holidays) after payment was due.

(c) A penalty of 10% of the above-mentioned amount due and unpaid (excluding the penalties in 5a and b above) if the delinquent payment is made between the 11th and 15th business days (excluding Saturday, Sundays and holidays) after payment was due.

(d) A penalty of 15% of the above-mentioned amount due and unpaid (excluding the penalties in 5a, b, and c above) if the delinquent payment is made between the 16th and 30th business days (excluding Saturday, Sunday and holidays) after payment was due.

(e) A penalty of 20% of the above-mentioned amount due and unpaid (excluding the penalties in 5a, b, c, and d above) if the delinquent payment is made between the 31st and 50th business day after the payment was due.

(f) Payments made after such 50th business day shall require in lieu of the said additional 20% payment, the payment of an additional amount equal to 50% (fifty per cent) of the initial amount payable plus an additional 10% payment for each thirty days after the 50th day in which payment is not

— 24 —

made. Such 50% and 10% payments shall not be required unless written notice has been given (which may not be given before the 31st day after the date of receipt of their completed billings and all necessary and completed W-4 forms) that the employer is delinquent and the employer has not made the payment within 15 business days after receipt of such notice.

(g) The above delinquent payment penalties shall not apply to payments which have not been made by the Company by reason of

> (i) A bona fide dispute as to the amount due and payable notice of which shall be filed within five business days following receipt of bills with the local of the Federation in whose jurisdiction the work was performed.

> (ii) Emergencies beyond the control of the Company.

> (iii) Where the Company inadvertently makes a less than full payment and presentation of the claim for the remainder is deliberately delayed in an attempt to collect a penalty.

(6) Sound Track Albums

Wage payments for record albums produced from theatrical motion picture and TV Film scores will be made within 45 working days of release of the album.

L. *Regulations Relating to Overdubbing, Tracking, Sweetening, Multiple Parts, etc.*

(a) Except as is specifically permitted below, nothing contained in this agreement shall be deemed to permit dubbing or tracking. The dubbing or tracking specifically permitted hereunder shall relate only to recordings made under, and during the term of, this agreement, subject to paragraph (g) on page 27.

(b) During a session the Company may add live performances to a recording made at the same session without notice and without any additional payment to the musicians employed for the session.

(c) After the completion of an original session the Company may add vocal performances to the recordings made at that original session without any additional payment to the musicians employed at the original session for their services thereat.

(d) At a session subsequent to the completion of the original session at which music was first recorded, the Company may add additional instrumental performances to such recorded music without any additional payment to the musicians employed at the original session for their services thereat.

(e) If a musician performs multiple instrument parts (other than doubles), or the same part of the musician is recorded in order to create the sound of additional instruments, he shall be paid the total of all payments which would otherwise have been payable had separate musicians been used for those parts.

(f) The following special provisions relate solely to "royalty artists" as such term is defined below:

(i) The rates set forth in sub-division (ii) below shall apply to each musician who is a "royalty artist," whether such musician plays multiple parts, doubles, over-dubs, or "sweetens." A "royalty artist" is a musician (a) who records pursuant to a phonograph record contract which provides for a royalty payable to such musician at a basic rate of at least 3% of the suggested retail list price of records sold (less deductions usual and customary in the trade) (for contracts entered into after November 1, 1977) or a substantially equivalent royalty, or (b) who plays as a member of (and not as a sideman with) a recognized self-contained group as defined in subdivision (iii).

(ii) For the first session at which such royalty artist performs in respect to each selection he shall receive the basic session rate per song.

(iii) A "recognized self-contained group" is:

(a) two or more persons who perform together in fields other than phonograph records under a group name (whether fictional or otherwise); and

(b) the members of which are recording pursuant to a phonograph record contract which provides for a royalty payable with respect to the group at a basic rate of at least 3% of the suggested retail list price of records sold (less deductions usual and customary in the trade) or a substantially equivalent royalty; and

(c) all of the musicians of which are or become members of the American Federation of Musicians as provided in this agreement.

Replacements of or additions to members of a recognized self-contained group shall be subject to the provisions of subdivision (i) and (ii) above, if they qualify under items (a), (b) and (c) of this subdivision (iii).

(iv) This subsection (f) shall not be applicable to any musician who himself is not a "royalty artist" but who nevertheless performs hereunder with such royalty artist or royalty artists.

(v) The provisions of this sub-paragraph shall not be applicable unless the contract between the royalty artists and the Company and all amendments thereto have been filed with the Office of the President of the Federation.

(g) The tracking permitted by the foregoing provisions of this agreement does not apply to recordings by symphonic orchestras. As to such recordings the Federation agrees to grant waivers which will permit tracking in any case needed to meet unusual situations subject only to the following procedures: (i) waiver requests will be made in advance of the intended use when it is known that tracking will be employed; and (ii) if not so requested, prompt notice of such use will be given to the Federation after the event. It is the specific understanding of the parties that tracking will continue to be permitted in those situations where tracking under prior agreements has heretofore been practiced.

M. *Certain Persons Not To Be Placed On Form B Contract*

A producer or any other person who acts in a Company capacity can be placed on the Form B contract only if he actually performs a musical service on that contract which is covered by this agreement. No contractor shall serve as an engineer, producer, or in any capacity representing the employer with respect to the session on which he is the contractor.

II

ARRANGERS, ORCHESTRATORS, COPYISTS

Arrangers, orchestrators and copyists shall be paid not less than the rates set forth below and the conditions set forth shall apply:

A. *Arrangers*

(1) Definition—Arranging is the art of preparing and adapting an already written composition for presentation in other than its original form. An arrangement shall include reharmonization, paraphrasing and/or development of a composition so that it fully represents the melodic, harmonic and rhythm structure and requires no changes or additions.

(2) Credits—Unless barred by a legal obligation undertaken by an arranger, he shall receive name credit on all seven-inch "pop single" records and on all tapes and cartridges in respect of which the number of arrangers used is six or less. Unless the arranger requests he not be given credit and if no legal obligation undertaken by him prevents the use of his name by the Company, the arranger shall receive name credit on all albums. Such credit may appear either on the record label or jacket, or on the tape or cartridge label or package.

(3) Minimum rates—Since arranging represents highly individual creative skills, the wages paid for arranging are left to the discretion of the person doing the work, provided, however, that the wages shall never be less than provided for in paragraph B. (3). Arranging shall be paid for in addition to orchestrating where the same person performs the work of the two classifications. Payment for making and orchestrating an arrangement shall cover both the minimum for arranging and orchestrating.

B. *Orchestrators*

(1) Definition—Orchestrating is the labor of scoring the various voices and/or instruments of an arrangement without changing or adding to the melodies, counter-melodies, harmonies and rhythms.

— 29 —

(2) Times rates for orchestrators—May be used only on takedowns, adjustments, alterations, additions and in other situations where page rates are impractical. The hourly rates for time work shall be $17.82 ($19.07 effective 11-1-80).

(3) Page rates for orchestrators [subject to the rules of paragraph "B. (4)"].

(a) For not more than ten lines per score page:

(i) Orchestrating an arrangement when incomplete material is furnished, per page, $11.18 ($11.96 effective 11-1-80).

(ii) Orchestrating an arrangement when complete material is furnished, per page, $5.62 ($6.01 effective 11-1-80).

(iii) Revoicing a score $5.62 ($6.01 effective 11-1-80).

(b) For each additional single iine in excess of ten lines per score page, $.49 ($.52 effective 11-1-80).

(c) For adding lines to a score already orchestrated (other than revoicing a score) when performed by the original orchestrator, per score page, per line, $.54 ($.58 effective 11-1-80). Any other orchestrator will be paid in accordance with (a) (ii), above.

(d) For adding piano part, in accordance with (a) (ii), above.

(e) Orchestrating the parts (without score), the combined rate for orchestrating and copying.

(f) For scoring a piano part from a lead or melody sheet, per piano page, $11.18 ($11.96 effective 11-1-80).

(g) For scoring a two-line or three-line full piano part from an orchestral score (or parts) or for scoring for solo piano, accordion, harp, etc., for individual performances, per piano page, $20.79 ($22.25 effective 11-1-80).

(h) For scoring for (choral) voices (a page to consist of not more than four voices, which may include a piano part, with come sopras being paid for),

Per four bar page ...... $4.91 ($5.25 effective 11-1-80)

Each additional voice .... $ .49 ($ .52 effective 11-1-80)

— 30 —

(4) The following rules shall apply to page rates:

(a) A score page consists of four bars and shall be computed on the basis of a minimum of ten lines.

(b) Double staff parts shall count as two lines.

(c) Each line of a divisi part shall count as one line.

(d) A pick-up shall be computed as a full measure.

(e) Come sopras shall be paid for.

(f) Repeats shall not be used within a chorus to reduce the wage paid (but repeats, del segno, and the like, which appear in the composition are permissible).

(g) The last page may be paid for on a half-page basis.

(h) The page rates do not include proofreading service.

(i) Voice and conductor lines written into a score shall be treated as instrumental lines.

(j) The word "piano" shall be deemed to include organ, harp, celeste, harpsichord, accordion, cymbalum, etc., when written on two staves.

C. *Copyists*

(1) Time rates for copyists—May be used only on pasting, cutting, production lines, and in other situations where page rates are impractical. The hourly rates for time work shall be $9.18 effective 11-1-79 and $9.82 effective 11-1-80.

(2) Page rates for copyists shall be as follows (subject to the rules set forth in paragraph "(C. (3)")):

INSTRUMENTAL PARTS:

	8% 11-1 79	7% 11-1 80
1. a. Single stave parts: single notation	$ 1.84	$ 1.97
b. Single stave parts: chorded and/or divisi	3.19	3.41
(Chorded: Guitar, banjo, vibraphone and similar parts) (Divisi: When more than 50% of page)		
2. a. Double stave parts: chorded piano, organ, harp, celeste, etc.	3.19	3.41
b. Rhythm piano parts: chord symbols and bass line	2.43	2.60
3. a. Piano with vocal melody cued (no lyrics—full chords)	4.16	4.45
b. Rhythm piano with vocal melody cued (no lyrics—chord symbols)	3.29	3.52
c. Piano with orchestral cues (Piano-Conductor)	5.08	5.44
4. a. Piano-Vocal: 3 staves with lyrics (one set) and full chords	4.86	5.20
b. Rhythm Piano-Vocal: 3 staves with lyrics (one set) and chord symbols	3.94	4.22
c. Piano-Vocal and orchestral cues/with lyrics (Piano-Conductor)	5.45	5.83
5. Lead Sheet: single melody line with lyrics (one set) and chord symbols	7.29	7.80
6. Concert score parts where transposition is necessary (no additional charge to be made for transposition)	2.75	2.94

VOCAL PARTS:

	8% 11-1 79	7% 11-1 80
7. a. Single voice line with lyrics (one set)	2.75	2.94
b. Foreign language lyrics, extra per page	.65	.70
8. a. Choir parts with lyrics (one set)	8.26	8.84
b. Foreign language lyrics, extra per page	.49	.52

CONDUCTOR PARTS:

(Piano-Conductor), Production, Control, etc. (one or more staves)

	11-1 79	11-1 80
9. a. Lead lines with notated instrumental cues	$10.10	$10.81
b. (+) Harmonically complete	13.72	14.68
(+) NOTE: If 12 stave paper is used in this category, not more than 3 braced systems per page shall be allowed.		
10. Adding lyrics (or words) per set, per page:		
a. Single stave parts	.65	.70
b. Multiple stave parts	.49	.52
c. Foreign language	1.03	1.10
11. Numbering bars, per page (no charge for normal use of rehearsal letters)	.27	.29
12. Chord symbols (when added, per page):		
a. Single stave parts	.65	.70
b. Multiple stave parts	.27	.29
13. a. Single stave part for SOLO PERFORMANCE	50% additional	
b. Solo piano, classical, concert, symphonic or similar parts	5.45	5.83
14. MASTER COPY FOR REPRODUCTION: Copying or extracting parts to be duplicated by any process—Double all applicable rates (except items 5, 8 a and b, 9 a and b above which shall be paid at the applicable single rate)	Double all applicable rates.	
15. Adding symbols (other than chord symbols) for Electronic Instruments or Devices		
a. Single stave parts	1.08	1.16
b. Multiple stave parts	.54	.58

(3) The following rules shall apply to page rates:

(a) For duplicating orchestra and band scores (note for note), the minimum rate shall be seventy-five (75%) per cent of the orchestrating rate for scoring same.

(b) For remaking a score from regular parts, the minimum rate shall be seventy-five (75%) per cent of the orchestrating rate for scoring same.

(c) Modulations, new introductions, endings and interpolations from piano shall be paid for at orchestrating rates.

(d) Symphony, opera, cantata, oratorio, ballet or any other standard or classical music (copies, transcriptions, extractions) shall be paid for at forty (40%) per cent more than the rates listed.

(e) Special routine work (writing only) where two or more scores or orchestral parts must be used or referred to in constructing overtures, selections, finales, etc., shall be paid for at fifty (50%) per cent more than the rates listed, provided that if such work requires a transposition of parts, for the parts so transposed, there shall be an extra charge of 50% of the listed rates.

(f) The contracting copyist shall be designated as a supervisor copyist and he shall be paid for his services 25% more than the wage scale for the work with respect to which he acts (including copying done by him) under the following circumstances:

  (i) when he is required by the Company to give out or collect work and to supervise and give instructions with respect to the assignments, or

  (ii) when the conditions of the job require the services of more than one copyist and the contracting copyist has notified the Company that more than one copyist will be required. Such notice, however, shall not be required when the copyist has received the work less than 72 hours prior to the recording session.

(g) When two or more copyists are required to split scores for the convenience of the Company, each copyist shall be paid at page and half-page rates for the section copied by him, but not less than the applicable hourly rate.

(h) Rates for copying do not include any proofreading services. Proofreading, if required by the Company, shall be paid for at the rate of $12.69 effective 11-1-79 and $13.58 effective 11-1-80 per hour, with no minimum call to be applicable to such rate.

(i) Editing shall be paid for at the copying rate plus 50%.

(j) Rates shall be computed on the basis of ten stave paper except that parts requiring three or more braced staves shall be written on twelve stave paper, unless impractical.

(k) Rates shall be computed on page and half-page rates except that the first page shall be paid in full rather than pro-rated.

(l) An average of four bars per stave shall be secured, if possible, and two staves of the first page (or any following pages, if necessary) shall be used for titles or other written items.

(m) The copyist who prepared the original part shall be paid the listed rate for any reproductions thereof by any mechanical means whatsoever except where a master copy was previously paid for at the rate listed.

(n) All paper and necessary working material shall be supplied by the Company or furnished by the copyist at cost.

(o) Transposition of all parts shall be paid for at fifty (50%) per cent more than the listed rates.

(p) Use of rehearsal letters every two, three or four bars or to circumvent payment for numbering shall not be deemed normal use.

D. *Health and Welfare Fund Contributions*

For each Arranger and Orchestrator the Company will contribute to any existing lawful Health and Welfare Fund of any Federation Local and commencing thirty days after notice in writing to any such lawful Fund as may be established hereafter by any other Federation Local, the sum of $2.60 for each original composition as to which services are performed on non-symphonic records performed within the jurisdiction of such Federation Local by each arranger and orchestrator covered by this agreement but not less than $3.75 nor more than $7.80 for any individual for all music services performed in respect to any one Form B contract.

For each Copyist the Company will contribute to any existing lawful Health and Welfare Fund of any Federation Local and commencing thirty days after notice in writing to any such lawful Fund as may be established hereafter by any other Federation Local, for work on non-symphonic records performed within the jurisdiction of such Federation Local by each copyist covered by this agreement, the sum of $3.00 per day, but not less than $3.75 for each original service, with a maximum of $15.00 per week.

With respect to any such composition as to which services are performed within the jurisdiction of a Federation Local where no such Fund is established, the Employer shall make the applicable payment to each such arranger, orchestrator, and copyist.

No such Health and Welfare Fund contribution whether paid to any Fund or paid directly to an arranger, orchestrator, and copyist shall be considered wages or the basis for computing the applicable AFM-EPW contribution or any other payments under this agreement such as overtime, premium pay, etc.

E. General rules applicable to arrangers, orchestrators, copyists and librarians

(1) The arranger or orchestrator shall deliver to the copyist a full score. A full score is a visual representation of parts to be performed by instruments and/or voice of a musical ensemble systematically placed on a series of staves, one above the other, and in which no other than two instruments are combined on a single staff. Abbreviations by come sopra and/or col indications within the same score may be used.

(2) Arrangements, orchestrations and parts previously made for a use other than phonograph records shall be paid for hereunder when first used for phonograph records. Arrangements, orchestrations and parts made initially for phonograph records shall not be used in any other field either by the

Company or with its authorization unless the rate applicable to such purposes is paid.

(3) Arrangers, orchestrators and copyists shall stamp the first and last pages of all arrangements and scores and the first page of all parts with their official union stamp. Card number, local and year must be written on deshon master copy.

(4) In cases where an hourly rate is applicable the minimum call shall be four hours, provided, however, that in the case of copyists the minimum shall be $45.

(5) Orchestrators and copyists shall receive the following premium rates:

(a) For work from 6:00 P.M. to 12 midnight, the listed rate plus one-half.

(b) For work on Saturdays from 9:00 A.M. to 6:00 P.M., the listed rate plus one-half.

(c) For work in excess of eight hours in one day and until midnight, the listed rate plus one-half.

(d) For work from 12 midnight until dismissed, and after 6:00 P.M. on Saturdays, double the listed rates.

(e) For work performed on the same job at anytime following a call-back less than eight hours after prior dismissal during premium pay hours, double the listed rates.

(f) For work on Sundays and the following holidays: New Year's Day, Lincoln's Birthday, Washington's Birthday, Memorial Day, Independence Day, Labor Day, Thanksgiving Day and Christmas Day double the listed rate.

Each of these holidays shall be observed on the day on which it is observed by employees of the United States Government or of the Government of Canada.

(6) (a) If the Company requests an orchestrator or copyist to work in a city other than the one in which he resides, work done out of town or en route shall be paid for at the listed rate plus 25%. In the case of an orchestrator, the Company shall guarantee a minimum of $65.00 per day plus $40.00 for personal

expenses. In the case of a copyist, the Company shall guarantee a minimum of $50.00 plus $40.00 for personal expenses. In addition, when such orchestrator or copyist is required to remain overnight, the Company will reimburse the musician for the reasonable cost of a hotel room.

(b) Round-trip first class transportation, with sleeper for overnight travel, shall be furnished by the Company.

(7) Pick up and messenger service will be paid for by the Company.

(8) The rates specified herein relate to arranging orchestrating and copying services of every nature as utilized in connection with phonograph records and no other rates shall be applied for any such services.

(9) Copyists and librarians who are required by the Company to attend recording sessions shall be paid at the page rate or at the hourly rate, whichever is higher.

(10) The leader or arranger shall collect and return musical parts and scores to the Company representatives at the end of each recording session, provided however, that the Company shall not be liable for the leader's or arranger's failure to collect such parts and scores if it did not interfere with his efforts to do so.

EXHIBIT B

PENSION WELFARE FUNDS

1. The Company shall contribute an amount equal to ten per cent (10%) of the earnings of persons covered by this agreement (except for the payments made in lieu of Health and Welfare Fund contributions under Exhibit A, I, A (6) and II, D, above, and under the Special Payments Fund Agreement attached as Exhibit C) computed at the minimum rates set forth in Exhibit A as follows:

   (a) For services performed in the United States to the American Federation of Musicians' and Employers' Pension Welfare Fund created by the Trust Indenture dated October 2, 1959, as heretofore or hereafter amended.

   (b) For services performed in the Dominion of Canada to the American Federation of Musicians' and Employers' Pension Welfare Fund created by the Agreement and Declaration of Trust dated April 9, 1962 as heretofore or hereafter amended.

   It is understood that, under the terms of said trust agreements, the employees (in addition to musicians as therein defined) on behalf of whom contributions to the aforesaid Funds may be made by other employers include the following:

   (i) full-time employees of the Funds themselves,

   (ii) full-time office and clerical employees of the Federation and any of its affiliated Locals, and

   (iii) duly elected officers and representatives of the Federation and of any of its affiliated Locals.

2. The Company shall make such payments to such place as the Trustees of the Funds may designate, upon the filing of a Form B contract.

3. The Company shall submit reports in such form as the Trustees may reasonably require; and the Company shall be subject to such reasonable audit by the Trustees as the Trustees may require.

4. The Federation and said Trustees, or either of them, may enforce any provision of this Exhibit B.

EXHIBIT C

PHONOGRAPH RECORD MANUFACTURERS'
SPECIAL PAYMENTS FUND AGREEMENT
(November, 1979)

AGREEMENT, made and delivered in the City and State of New York, on the date set forth below, by and between the undersigned and such others as shall hereafter agree to contribute to the fund referred to hereafter (individually called "first party" and collectively "first parties"), the undersigned Administrator ("Administrator"), and The American Federation of Musicians of the United States and Canada ("Federation").

WITNESSETH:

(a) Each first party has executed and delivered this agreement pursuant to its undertaking so to do as provided by the Phonograph Record Labor Agreement (November, 1979), simultaneously herewith entered into with the Federation.

(b) Each first party by executing and delivering this Agreement assumes the duties and obligations to be performed and undertaken by each such first party hereunder. The Administrator has been designated collectively by the first parties, who have requested it to assume and perform the duties of Administrator hereunder, and it is willing to do so in the manner prescribed herein.

NOW, THEREFORE, in consideration of the premises, of the mutual covenants herein contained, of the undertakings assumed by each first party, and of the undertakings herein by the Administrator at the request of the first parties, it is agreed as follows:

1.   (a) There are incorporated herein and made part hereof, as though fully set forth herein, Addendums A and B.

(b) Subject to paragraph 2(d) hereof, each first party to this Agreement shall make the payments to the Administrator called for in Addendum A hereto, to provide for

(i) said First Party's contribution to the musicians' share of the Fund as defined under paragraph 2(b) hereof, and

(ii) any employment taxes or insurance premiums which may be owing by the First Parties with respect to the distribution of the musicians' share of the Fund.

— 40 —

(c) Within forty-five (45) days after the end of each calendar half-year (that is within forty-five (45) days after December 31 and June 30th in each year), each first party will pay to the Administrator such portion of the aforesaid payments as may have accrued hereunder during the preceding half-year, provided that the Administrator may agree with any first party that semi-annual payments be made with respect to other half-yearly periods ending on dates satisfactory to the Administrator. Each payment hereunder shall be accompanied by a statement, certified by the Treasurer, Controller, or other authorized officer or representative of the first party making such payment, containing such information as may reasonably be required to ascertain the correctness of the payment made. If such payments are not made when due hereunder, the same shall bear interest at the rate of six per cent (6%) per annum from the date when such payment was due.

(d) Each first party at all times, without limitation to the duration of this Agreement, shall keep full and accurate records and accounts concerning all transactions on which payments to the Administrator are based pursuant to this Agreement, in convenient form and pursuant to approved and recognized accounting practices. The Administrator shall have the right from time to time, without limitation to the duration of this Agreement and at all reasonable times during business hours, to have its duly authorized agents examine and audit such records and accounts, and such other records and accounts as may be necessary, such examination and audit to be made for the purpose of verifying any statements made hereunder by each first party, or due from such first party, during a period not exceeding four (4) years preceding such examination and of determining the amount of payments due to the Administrator pursuant hereto. It is agreed that the four year period provided herein shall not effect the operation of the applicable statute of limitations. Each first party agrees to afford all necessary facilities to such authorized agents to make such examination and audit and to make such extracts and excerpts from said records and accounts as may be necessary or proper according to approved and recognized accounting practices. Examinations and audits made pursuant hereto

— 41 —

shall be coordinated, to the extent practicable, with examinations and audits made under the Phonograph Record Trust Agreements to which first party is signatory so that inconvenience to the first party may be minimized.

(e) Any sale, assignment, lease or license of, or other transfer of title to, or permission to use any device covered by Addendum A to this Agreement whether by operation of law or otherwise, shall be subject to the rights and duties established by this Agreement. The Administrator shall be advised monthly of each purchaser, assignee, lessee, licensee, transferee or user and of the identity of the phonograph record (as defined above) involved. No sale, assignment, lease, license, transfer or permission shall be made or granted by any first party to any person, firm or corporation doing business within the United States, Canada, or Puerto Rico, unless and until such purchaser, assignee, lessee, licensee, transferee, or user, shall become an additional first party hereto. No other sale, assignment, lease, license, transfer or permission shall be made or granted unless such purchaser, assignee, lessee, licensee, transferee, or user, shall promise to make to such first party the payments required by this Agreement, which said first party shall pay over to the Administrator, but only to the extent that such first party has received such payments (i) in the United States or Canada, or (ii) in United States or Canadian currency or in a currency convertible into United States or Canadian currency, or (iii) in a currency not convertible into United States or Canadian currency, of which such first party has made beneficial use, or (iv) in an asset other than currency. No such first party will, without the consent of the Administrator and Federation forgive or compromise such obligation.

(f) All payments and other communications for each first party to the Administrator shall be made to the Administrator at its office which shall be located in New York, N.Y.

2. (a) The Administrator accepts the duties hereby assigned to it, and shall establish the proper administrative machinery and processes necessary for the performance of its duties hereunder. The Administrator shall as soon as practicable after May first of each year distribute as herein provided

the "musicians' share of the Fund," as defined in paragraph 2 (b) hereof. Each musician, as collectively referred to in paragraph 1 of the Phonograph Record Labor Agreement (November, 1979), shall receive as a special payment a fraction of the total distribution which shall be determined as follows: the numerator of said fraction shall be a sum determined by adding the scale wages payable to such musician by all First Parties hereto (i) during the immediately preceding calendar year weighted or multiplied by 5, (ii) during the immediately preceding calendar year less one weighted or multiplied by 4, (iii) during the immediately preceding calendar year less two weighted or multiplied by 3, (iv) during the immediately preceding calendar year less three weighted or multiplied by 2, and (v) during the immediately preceding calendar year less four weighted or multiplied by 1; the denominator of said fraction shall be a sum determined by adding the scale wages payable to all such musicians during the same calendar years as aforesaid by all said First Parties hereto similarly weighted or multiplied as set forth above. In the case of arrangers and orchestrators scale wages for all purposes of this paragraph 2 (a) shall be deemed to be 150% of the scale wages paid to an instrumentalist for each tune on which the arranger or orchestrator performed services hereunder.

By way of illustration but not limitation:

Example 1:

If the scale wages payable to a musician participating in the 1971 distribution have been $50 in 1970 and $100 in 1969 and the total scale wages payable to all musicians during the same two years have been $10,000 in 1970 and $9,000 in 1969 the fraction of the distribution payable to that musician would be determined as follows:

Musician's scale wages	*Total scale wages*
Year	
1970 — $ 50 × 5 = $250	$10M × 5 = $50M
1969 — 100 × 4 = 400	9M × 4 = 36M
$650	$86,000

— 43 —

The musician's 1971 special payment would be 650/86000 of the "musicians' share of the Fund."

Example 2:

If the scale wages payable to a musician participating in the 1975 distribution have been $50 in 1974, $100 in 1973, $70 in 1972, none in 1971, and $30 in 1970 and if the total scale wages payable to all musicians during the same five years have been $10,000 in 1974, $9,000 in 1973, $7,000 in 1972, $5,000 in 1971 and $5,000 in 1970, the fraction of the distribution payable to that musician would be determined as follows:

	Musician's scale wages	*Total scale wages payable to all musicians*
Year		
1974 —	$ 50 × 5 = $250	$10M × 5 = $50M
1973 —	100 × 4 = 400	9M × 4 = 36M
1972 —	70 × 3 = 210	7M × 3 = 21M
1971 —	0 × 2 = 0	5M × 2 = 10M
1970 —	30 × 1 = 30	5M × 1 = 5M
	$890	$122,000

The musician's 1975 special payment would be 890/122,000 of the "musicians' share of the Fund."

(b) For purposes of this agreement, the "musician's share of the Fund" shall be an amount equal to:

(i) all sums received by the Administrator up to May first of the year of distribution, with respect to sales of phonograph records made:

(A) during the preceding calendar year, or,

(B) at any time prior to the preceding calendar year, if the payment with respect to such sales, was received by the Administrator after May first of the preceding calendar year.

(ii) less:

(A) all expenses reasonably incurred in the administration of the Fund, including the compensation of the Administrator herein provided, and appropriate bonding premiums.

(B) amounts reasonably reserved by the Administrator as an operating Fund, and for contingencies, and,

(C) an amount (hereinafter referred to as the "manufacturers' share of the Fund") equal to the total of any social security tax, Federal and/or State Unemployment Insurance Tax, other employment taxes, Disability Insurance premiums, and/or Workmen's Compensation premiums, which may be owing by the First Parties, individually or collectively, and/or by the Administrator, as employer or employers, with respect to the distribution of the musicians' share of the Fund.

(c) The First Parties, individually and collectively, hereby irrevocably designate the Administrator as their agent to pay from the manufacturers' share of the Fund, any social security tax, Federal and/or State Unemployment Insurance Tax, other employment taxes, Disability Insurance premiums, and/or Workmen's Compensation premiums, which may be owing by the First Parties individually and/or collectively, as employer or employers, with respect to the distribution of the musicians' share of the Fund.

(d) Notwithstanding any other provisions of this agreement, a First Party may, at the time it makes its annual payment to the Fund, request that the Administrator refund to it such proportion of such payment as:

(i) the total of any taxes and insurance premiums which may be payable under Paragraph 2(b) (ii) (C) hereof, with respect to the distribution of the musicians' share of the Fund in the year of payment, bears to

(ii) the total payments made to the Fund by First Parties in said year.

Any such refund shall be made by the Administrator to the First Party requesting the refund not later than September first of the year of payment.

If a refund is made to a First Party under this subparagraph, the Administrator shall not be responsible in said year, for payment of said First Party's share of any taxes and insurance premiums payable under Paragraph 2(b) (ii) (C) hereof, with regard to the distribution of the musicians' share of the Fund.

(e) The Federation has agreed to furnish to the Administrator, and to cause its local unions to furnish to the Administrator, all data in the possession or subject to the control thereof which is necessary and proper to assist in the orderly and accurate distribution to musicians as provided herein and to request the Trustees of the American Federation of Musicians and Employers' Pension Welfare Fund to do likewise upon reimbursement of all costs reasonably incurred thereby in so doing.

(f) The Administrator shall indemnify and hold the First Parties harmless out of the Fund against any liability for making any of the payments to the musicians under paragraph 2(a) hereof or any payments of employment taxes and insurance premiums which may be required to be made by the Administrator under paragraph 2(c) hereof, it being the express intent of the parties that all such payments are to be made out of the Fund with no further cost or expense of any kind whatsoever to the First Parties. Without limitation of the foregoing, the Administrator also shall furnish a surety bond with a responsible surety company satisfactory to the First Parties and to the Federation, to guarantee the full and faithful performance of its duties as herein described.

(g) In making distribution to musicians hereunder, the Administrator shall clearly and legibly display the following legend on all checks, vouchers, letters or documents of transmittal: "This is a special payment to you by all of the Phonograph Record Labor Agreements negotiated by the American Federation of Musicians."

(h) In the event of the death of a musician entitled to a distributive share hereunder, the Administrator shall distribute such share to the beneficiary designated by such musician pursuant to the AFM-EPW Pension Welfare Fund; and if no beneficiary be so designated, then to the surviving spouse of such musician; and if there be no such person, to the musician's estate.

(i) If a musician for whom a distributive share has been set apart cannot be found or if payment under this Agreement has been tendered but is not completed after efforts which the Administrator deems reasonable, the Administrator shall add such amounts to a reserve Fund and hold the same therein pending receipt of claim or until the end of the second full calendar year following the first day of May when such amounts became payable. Thereafter, all such amounts remaining unclaimed shall be redeposited in the "musicians' share of the Fund" as defined in paragraph 2(b) for distribution as therein provided.

3. (a) In the event that any First Party shall default in the payment of any sums to the Administrator when the same shall become due pursuant to this Agreement, the Administrator shall have the duty, right and power forthwith to commence action or to take any other proceedings as shall be necessary for the collection thereof, including the power and authority to compromise and settle with the Federation's consent. The Administrator's reasonable expenses, attorney's fees and other disbursements incurred in the collection of any such overdue sums shall be paid to the Administrator by the First Party so defaulting and such payment shall be added to the special payment fund.

(b) Nothing contained herein shall create any cause of action in favor of any musician as defined in the Phonograph Record Labor Agreement (November, 1979) against any First Party but the Federation may enforce distribution of the musicians' share of the Fund in behalf of the individual musicians.

(c) The Administrator shall deposit all money and property received by it, with or without interest, with any bank or trust company, insured by the Federal Deposit Insurance Corporation and having capital, surplus and undivided profits exceeding $5,000,000; provided, however, that in the event that Canadian dollars are receivable by the Administrator and it is not feasible or desirable to convert such Canadian dollars into the United States funds, such Canadian funds and any securities purchased therewith may be deposited in a Chartered

Bank of the Dominion of Canada, anything herein to the contrary notwithstanding. Except as modified by the provisions of paragraph 3(d) hereof, the Administrator shall have the right and power to invest and reinvest the said money and property only in bonds and other direct obligations of the United States of America and of the Dominion of Canada, without regard to the proportion which any such investment or investments may bear to the entire amount of the Fund and to sell, exchange and otherwise deal with such investments as the Administrator may deem desirable.

(d) In connection with the collection of any sums due to it hereunder, the Administrator may consent to and participate in any composition of creditors, bankruptcy, reorganization or similar proceeding, and in the event that as a result thereof the Administrator shall become the holder of assets other than money, obligations to pay money conditioned only as to the time of payment, or property of the class specified in paragraph 3(c) hereof (which assets are in this subsection (d) called "property"), the Administrator may consent to and participate in any plan of reorganization, consolidation, merger, combination, or other similar plan, and consent to any contract, lease, mortgage, purchase, sale or other action by any corporation pursuant to such plan and accept any property which might be received by the Administrator under any such plan, whether or not such property is of the class in which the Administrator by paragraph 3(c) hereof, is authorized to invest the Fund; the Administrator may deposit any such property with any protective, reorganization or similar committee, delegate discretionary power thereto, and pay part of its expenses and compensation and any assessment levied with respect to such property; the Administrator may exercise all conversions, subscription, voting and other rights of whatsoever nature pertaining to any such property, and grant proxies, discretionary or otherwise, in respect thereof and accept any property which may be acquired by the Administrator by the exercise of any such rights, whether or not such property is of the class in which the Administrator, by paragraph 3(c) hereof, is authorized to invest the Fund. Anything to the contrary contained in this paragraph 3(d) notwithstanding, the Administrator shall reasonably endeavor to dispose of any such property in order that the Fund, to the fullest extent possible, at all times shall be comprised as specified in paragraph 3(c) hereof.

(e) Parties dealing with the Administrator shall not be required to look to the application of any moneys paid to the Administrator.

(f) The Administrator has consented to act as Administrator hereunder upon the express understanding that it shall not in any event or under any circumstances be liable for any loss or damage resulting from anything done or omitted in good faith, and further, that this understanding shall not be limited or restricted by any reference to or inference from any general or special provisions herein contained or otherwise. In particular, and without limiting the foregoing, the Administrator shall not be subject to any personal liability for moneys received and expended in accordance with the provisions hereof.

(g) Within ninety (90) days after the end of each calendar year, the Administrator shall furnish a statement for such calendar year of its operations to each First Party hereto making payments to the Administrator and to the Federation. Such statements shall set forth in detail the properties and moneys on hand and the operations of the Administrator during the immediately preceding calendar year, including without limitation the details of any compromise or settlement made by the Administrator with any First Party, and such other information and data as shall be appropriate to inform fully the recipients of such statements and shall be certified by independent certified public accountant.

(h) The Administrator, at all times without limitation to the duration of this Agreement, shall keep full and accurate records and accounts concerning all transactions involving the receipt and expenditure of moneys hereunder and the investment and reinvestment thereof, all in convenient form and pursuant to approved and recognized accounting practices.

Each First Party and the Federation shall have the right from time to time, without limitation to the duration of this agreement, and at all reasonable times during business hours, to have their respective duly authorized agents examine and audit the Administrator's records and accounts for the purpose of verifying any statements and payments made by the Administrator pursuant to this Agreement, during a period not exceeding two (2) years preceding such examination. The Administrator shall afford all necessary facilities to such authorized agents to make such examination and audit and to make extracts and excerpts from said records and accounts as may be necessary or proper according to approved and recognized accounting practices.

(i) The Administrator shall recognize and honor lawful assignments to the Federation of a portion of the payments to which any musician shall become entitled hereunder.

4. The compensation of the Administrator shall be as set forth in Addendum B hereto attached, and shall be paid out of the funds and property in the hands of the Administrator.

5. (a) The Administrator may resign at any time by thirty (30) days' written notice to the First Parties and the Federation. A successor Administrator shall thereupon be appointed by the Secretary of Labor of the United States.

(b) The Administrator shall be subject to removal as provided below, if an individual, the Administrator shall become unable to perform his duties hereunder by reason of illness or other incapacity or if the Administrator shall be guilty of malfeasance or neglect of duty hereunder. Any demand for the removal of the Administrator for the reasons aforesaid shall be submitted by any two or more of the First Parties hereto who have made individual payments hereunder to the Administrator during the calendar year immediately preceding the date of such submission aggregating $50,000 or more, together with the Federation, to the American Arbitration Association in New York, N.Y. The determination of whether the Administrator shall be removed for the reasons aforesaid shall be made in New York, N.Y. by three (3) Arbitrators selected from panels of the American Arbitration

Association in accordance with the Rules thereof and judgment upon the award rendered by the Arbitrators may be entered in any court having jurisdiction thereof.

(c) In the event of the death of the Administrator, if an individual, or the removal of the Administrator, a successor Administrator shall be appointed in the manner designated in paragraph 5(a) hereof.

(d) No Administrator under this Agreement shall be a representative of labor, or of any union, or of employees within the meaning of Section 302(b) of the Labor Management Relations Act, 1947.

6.   Any person, firm, corporation, association or other entity may apply to become an additional First Party to this Agreement by executing and delivering to the Administrator three (3) counterparts of Schedule 1 hereto attached. The Administrator shall indicate acceptance of such application by appropriately completing such application, executing such three (3) counterparts, and delivering one (1) such counterpart to such additional First Party at the Administrator's office in the City of New York and one (1) such counterpart to the Federation. The Administrator shall forthwith advise the Federation of the execution and delivery of such agreement, and shall regularly advise all other First Parties thereof.

7.   This Agreement shall be governed, construed and regulated in all respects by the laws of the State of New York.

IN WITNESS WHEREOF, each First Party, the Administrator and the Federation have hereunto set their respective names and seals, or have caused these presents to be executed by a duly authorized officer or officers thereof and their corporate seals affixed thereto as of the date set forth below.

Date   *Signatory*

ADDENDUM A

1. For the purposes of this Agreement, the terms "phonograph record" and "record" shall include phonograph records, wire or tape recordings, or other devices reproducing sound, and the term "master record" shall include any matrix, "mother," stamper or other device from which another such master record, phonograph record, wire or tape recording, or other device reproducing sound, is produced, reproduced, pressed or otherwise processed.

2. Each First Party shall make payments to the Administrator in the amounts computed as stated below, with respect to the sale during the period specified in 6 below of phonograph records, produced from master records containing music which was performed or conducted by musicians covered by, or required to be paid pursuant to, a collective bargaining agreement with the Federation known as Phonograph Record Labor Agreement (November, 1979) (but specifically excluding services solely as arranger, orchestrator or copyist) where such phonograph records are sold during said period by such First Party, or, subject to the provisions of paragraph 1(e) of the main text of this Agreement, by purchasers, lessees, licensees, transferees, or other users deriving title, lease, license, or permission thereto, by operation of law or otherwise, by, from or through such First Party.

3. The payments to the Administrator shall be computed as follows:

(a) .6% of the manufacturer's suggested retail price of each record, when such price does not exceed $3.79.

(b) For records where the manufacturer's suggested retail price exceeds $3.79, .58% of the manufacturer's suggested retail list price and for wire or tape recordings or other devices .5% of the manufacturer's suggested retail price.

With respect to a phonograph record produced after October 31, 1977, both from master records described in paragraph 2 of this Addendum A and recorded under Phonograph Record Labor Agreement (November, 1979) for which payments are due hereunder and from other master records, First Party shall pay that proportion of the amount provided for above as the number of such master records recorded under said Agreement bears to the total number of master records embodied in the phonograph record.

4. For the purpose of computing payments to the Administrator,

(a) Each First Party will report 100% of net sales;

(b) Each First Party will have a packaging allowance in the country of manufacture or sale of 15% of the suggested retail list price for phonograph records (other than for records where the manufacturer's suggested retail list price is $3.79 or less, and other than for singles in plain wrapping or sleeves) and 25% of the suggested retail list price for tapes and cartridges.

(c) Each First Party will have an allowance, with respect to "free" records, tapes and cartridges actually distributed, regardless of mix, (except for record clubs which are dealt with separately below), of up to 20% of the total records distributed;

(d) With respect to its record clubs, if any, each First Party will have an allowance of "free" and "bonus" records, tapes and cartridges actually distributed of up to 50% of the total records, tapes and cartridges distributed by or through the clubs; and with respect to such "free" and "bonus" records, tapes and cartridges, distributed by its clubs in excess thereof, each First Party will pay the full rate on 50% of the excess of such "free" and "bonus" records, tapes and cartridges so distributed.

5. Schedules of current manufacturer's suggested retail prices for each record in each First Party's catalogue shall be furnished by each First Party to the Administrator upon the execution and delivery of this Agreement and amendments and additions thereto shall be so furnished as and when established. For the purposes of determining the amounts payable hereunder, such suggested retail prices shall be computed exclusive of any sales or excise taxes on the sale of phonograph records subject to this Agreement. If any First Party discontinues the practice of publishing manufacturers' suggested retail prices, it agrees that it will negotiate a new basis for

computing payments hereunder which shall be equivalent to those required above.

6. The payments provided for in this Agreement shall be made with respect to the sales of any phonograph record produced from a master record described in paragraph 2 of this Addendum A which take place during the period commencing with the calendar year during which a phonograph record produced from such master record is first released for sale and terminating at the end of the tenth calendar year thereafter. The year of such release shall be counted as the first year of the ten years. (By way of illustration but not limitation, if a phonograph record produced from a master record made pursuant to Phonograph Record Labor Agreement (April, 1969), is first released for sale in May, 1969, payments shall be made with respect to sales of said record which take place during the calendar years 1969-1978 inclusive. If said phonograph record is first released for sale in February, 1972, payments shall be made with respect to sales of said record which take place during the calendar year 1972-1981 inclusive.)

7. The report to the Administrator required in paragraph 1(c) of the main text of this Agreement shall show the number of phonograph records, tapes and other devices subject to payment under this Agreement which have been sold during the period to be covered by the report, the dates of initial release for sale thereof, the manufacturer's suggested retail price thereof and of the component units thereof and the excise and sales taxes, if any, borne by the First Party thereon.

8. Despite anything to the contrary contained in this Agreement, it is specifically agreed that the First Party reserves the right, by written notice to the Administrator, effective with the effective date of any termination, modification, extension or renewal of the said Phonograph Record Labor Agreement (November, 1979), to terminate or change any of the terms of this Special Payments Fund Agreement, but no such termination or change shall be effective unless the First Party has secured the prior written approval thereto by the Federation. It is agreed, however, that no such change may have any retroactive effect.

— 54 —

9. Anything to the contrary herein contained notwithstanding, it is agreed that if the Phonograph Record Labor Agreement (November, 1979), or any successor agreement is not renewed or extended at or prior to its expiration date, and if a work stoppage by members of the Federation ensues, then all payments otherwise due to the Administrator based on sales for the period of such work stoppage, and only for such period, shall not be made to the Administrator. In lieu thereof, equivalent amounts shall be paid by each First Party as an additional contribution to the Trustee under the Phonograph Record Trust Agreement (November, 1979) unless otherwise determined as a condition for the cessation of such work stoppage.

ADDENDUM B

Administrator's Compensation

The total compensation of the Administrator for services rendered pursuant to this agreement and pursuant to similar agreements with producers and/or distributors of phonograph records and/or electrical transcriptions shall be at the total rate of Ten Thousand Dollars ($10,000) per annum.

SCHEDULE 1

Date:_____, 19____

The undersigned, desiring to become an additional First Party to the within Agreement, does hereby adopt the declarations of the First Parties set forth therein, does hereby make the request made by the First Parties therein, and in consideration of the undertakings assumed therein by each First Party and of the undertakings assumed therein by the Administrator at the request of the First Parties, does hereby request the Administrator to accept the undersigned as an additional First Party to such Agreement, and does assume and agrees to be bound by the terms, covenants and conditions to be performed thereunder.

_____
(Name of Company or Individual Signatory)

By_____
(Signature of Officer and Title)

Address:_____

_____

ACCEPTED:

United States Trust Company of New York

By_____
Vice-President
Administrator

(If executed in the Province of Quebec this Agreement shall be properly notarized and otherwise executed according to the laws of the Province.)

Index

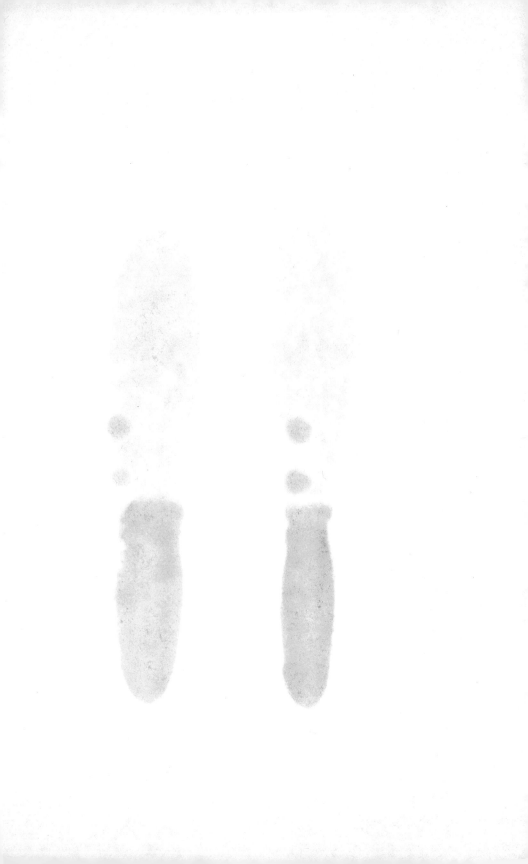

DATE DUE			
MAR 1 3 1984			
APR 2 6 1988			
FEB 1 1 92			
MAY 8 92			
FEB 1 3 1996			
APR 1 6 1997			

Concordia College Library
Bronxville, NY   10708